Creation Stories

Creation Stories

Landscapes and the Human Imagination

ANTHONY AVENI

Yale UNIVERSITY PRESS

New Haven and London

Published with assistance from the foundation established
in memory of Philip Hamilton McMillan of the Class of 1894,
Yale College.

Yale University Press books may be purchased in quantity for
educational, business, or promotional use. For information, please
e-mail sales.press@yale.edu (U.S. office) or
sales@yaleup.co.uk (U.K. office).

Set in Minion type by Integrated Publishing Solutions.
Printed in the United States of America.

Library of Congress Control Number: 2020943122
ISBN 978-0-300-25124-1 (hardcover : alk. paper)

A catalogue record for this book is available from the
British Library.

This paper meets the requirements of ANSI/NISO Z39.48-1992
(Permanence of Paper).

10 9 8 7 6 5 4 3 2 1

For Joe Calamia:
you and your bright ideas

Contents

Contents

PART FIVE

EXTREMES

Preface

Mountain valleys formed by the beating wings of a gigantic bird, islands pulled up from the ocean floor by a fisherman god with a magic hook, the sea bottom carved out by swordfish monsters, people-animals living in a mirror-image world beneath our feet, and the carcass of a giant transformed into the landscape we see today. These striking visual images were created in the minds of some of the world's most imaginative storytellers.

For most of human history, people have thought of nature and culture as one, and the universe as a distinct whole with all its parts and processes bound together, influencing one another. Careful observers of the world conjured up stories of creation as a way of addressing life's most basic questions: Where did it all come from? How did it begin? How do we fit into the picture? Storytellers sought ways to explain history, politics, social relations, and ideas about life after death in ways that made sense to them, if not to us. Listeners came to understand themselves as mediators in a powerful universal discourse. At stake lay the battle between fate and free will, body and soul.

Creation Stories celebrates this audacity of the human imagination. It explores the ground where myth and science meet by recounting creation narratives from a variety of cultures, past and present—stories that demonstrate humankind's universal, continuing fascination with the rhythms of the natural world. As we'll see, contemporary science's tale seems different from the others because it is guided by the particular path of history Western civilization has trod, but it too shares motifs with other creation stories. These overlapping narrative ideas remind us that there is a common denominator that unites us all—the desire for order, for pattern, in the world around us.

Creation Stories

About Storytelling

It is break time at a prison yard, and a handful of prisoners are seated in a circle—their daily custom. One inmate utters the number "168" and everyone chuckles. A second retorts "651," and once again laughter bubbles up. On a roll, he follows with "305," eliciting a more robust response—a few in the group even double over. The curious game continues for another ten minutes before a horn signals the end of the break.

One day a new recruit joins the conclave. As blurted-out numbers evoke reactions ranging from giggles to guffaws, he looks puzzled. Later, after the prisoners return to their cells, the perplexed newcomer asks his cellmate: "Hey, what's with all that number stuff?" His roomie responds: "Oh, that. We're just telling old stories. Most of us are lifers, no contact with the outside world, so they tend to be the same old jokes. Not much time to tell them, so we decided to organize—give each one a number and memorize them. All the one hundreds are animal stories, two hundreds are about marriage and divorce, and like that. I've got a list if you want to tell one sometime," he says. He rummages through his things and hands his companion a thick sheaf of papers.

A month goes by before the new guy feels he's ready for

his storytelling debut. As the group sits around in the noonday sun for their precious fifteen minutes of joke-telling, which opens with the well-received "183"—about the two dogs arguing over proprietorship of a fire hydrant—the novice seizes the moment and abruptly chimes in with "185" (an elm tree replacing the hydrant). No reaction—not even a smile. Undaunted, he changes the subject with "273." Dead silence. Three more vocal thrusts, each a little less heartfelt than the last, yield the same disappointing outcome. Glumly returning to his cell, the dejected detainee flops into his lower berth, sighs, and turns to his mate: "I don't get it. When you told '273' last week all the guys cracked up. Same deal with '185.' What happened with my '185'? What did I do wrong?" Following a painful pause and a grimace, the cellmate tells it like it is: "Face it. Some guys know how to tell a story and some just don't."

We can think of a story, writes Ferris Jabr in *Harper's* magazine, as "a choreographed hallucination that temporarily displaces reality." Stories have lives of their own: "They compel us to share them and, once told, they begin to grow and change.... They compete with one another for attention—for the opportunity to reach as many minds as possible. They find each other, intermingle, and multiply."[1] Most effective stories are adaptable, and those skilled at telling them know how to alter characters and sets to appeal to a range of audiences—or what anthropologists call mythic substitution. Take the highland Andean story of the constellation of the llama and her *cria* (baby) being stalked by a fox. When the tale spread eastward into the tropical rainforest of the Amazon basin, the carnivore predator fox became a jaguar who chases the herbivore prey, a tapir, across the sky. When it migrated to the foothills between the two ecozones, the tapir was replaced by a deer. Farther south in the Gran Chaco grasslands of southern Chile and Argentina, the constellation pair became a dog and a rhea, or South American ostrich—only this time, because of the ostrich's long neck (much like a llama's), pursuer and pursued switched positions in the sky.

Stories of creation are commonly termed myths, but the word "myth" carries a double-barreled definition that bothers me. On the one hand, it's just a story—a traditional story that often addresses a natural phenomenon and involves supernatural beings; on the other hand, a myth is also defined as a false belief based on fantasy or delusion, an "all made up" form of thinking. In that second sense, myth translates as a veiled or fabricated truth, a product of the fanciful imagination waiting to be debunked by science and replaced with *real* truth. But for people who tell their myths to relate events they experience to beliefs and practices in their daily lives, myths capture a valid and essential truth of the human experience. Take, for example, seasonal festivals like Dies Natalis Solis Invicti (birthday of the unconquered sun), the Roman celebration of the winter solstice. The story behind the holiday likely descends from the fifteenth-century BCE tale of Mithra, the Indo-Iranian god of light who ventures annually among the constellations of the zodiac. Ever watchful and protective of all who dwell below, he requires people to ask him to renew himself at his lowest point.

Such solstice-based festivals have been recognized around the world and endure even today as a time to rejoice that the sun god has reached his critical turning point low in the winter sky. Indeed, it seems that every culture in the world recognizes and celebrates the advent of the seasonal return of natural light at the very time when they need it most—in the dead of winter. Early Christians adapted the Roman Dies Natalis to tell a story about the birth of their Savior, the one who brings light to the world. The climax comes with his death and resurrection

during their Easter holiday. And although I would not consider myself a religious person, I too feel joy when, after a long,
hard winter, I bear witness to the days warming up, the snow
melting, and the first green plants sprouting in my front yard,
all thanks to the increasing radiance that occurs when the sun
has passed the winter solstice. Do my feelings—my unreasoned
response to the great solar turnabout—hold no truth? Don't
the seasonal symbols—what we eat, what we say, sing, or do—
convey the reality of our experience of the renewal of light that
happens when the sun alters its course in the spring? So let's
lose that second definition of myth. The stories of creation I'll
recount here are not just "all made up."

I think individuals trained in science pay too little attention to
stories of creation other than their own "Big Bang." They gen-
erally regard stories from other cultures about the creation of
the world as naïve because those tales imagine a universe that
mirrors the experiences of the human or animal world. They
differ from the Big Bang narrative about a universe that exists
for its own sake—a universe that scientists can observe and
test, and, depending on the results, revise their interpretation
about what's *really* going on. Some conclude that because the
ancients didn't understand the true nature of the various natural phenomena they observed, they developed myths that gave
them easy explanations. Other scientifically trained scholars
suggest that our human ancestors lacked the benefit of our
technology and the accumulated wisdom of the ages, so they
simply misread the environment, populated it with needless
spirits, and based their childlike interpretations of it on false
premises. In most scientifically trained minds, the idea that all
nature is endowed with life, that it consists of properties trans-
ferable to people, and that every material object acts according
to its own will, has little value—no matter how effective such

creation stories might be in guiding the everyday lives of those who tell them.

Those who attempt to assign myth a rational label, however, miss the essential point. For what makes the tales we'll encounter in this book so different from modern science's Big Bang story of creation is the human search for meaning and purpose. People participate in these creation stories: they engage in dialogue with supernaturals; they sacrifice, hoping for favors or mercy; they conduct rituals that retell their creation myth in order to secure their roles in a great human drama set on a cosmic stage. And they use imagery, as well as the grammar of poetry—analogy and metaphor—to tell their tales.

By contrast, the modern scientific story, with its central theme of a cataclysmic event that happened billions of years ago and brought everything into existence, describes the aftermath of a colossal cataclysmic drama over which we have no control. It includes the microcosmic seeds that would eventually become us—but we receive no credit line in the cast of characters. We write ourselves out of the script. With this scientific story, we can only document the changing condition of a universe that exists *for itself*. Our modern creation narrative comes equipped with no clues that pertain to the search for human meaning. And unlike mythology, it uses the abstract geometrical language of science to make its case. Modern scientists, for example, would tell a very different story about the Dies Natalis. They might construct illustrative charts showing the variation in the number of hours of daylight through the winter months and calculate the insolation (the quantity of solar energy on a unit of landscape at various latitudes, at different times of day and on different dates). Their story line could correlate these data with the times of germination of various plants, the end of the hibernation of bears and beavers, daily temperature maxima and minima, rainfall records, and so on. Out of this collection of truths quantitatively arrived at, there would emerge a deity-free, rational version of the story of the solar orb's seasonal turning.

In the opinion of the best-selling storyteller Alan Watts, there are four basic questions about origins that people have asked through the ages: Who started it? Are we going to make it? Where are we going to put it? And who's going to clean up?[2] Recast as the proverbial "five W's" of journalism, the burning questions might be, Who am I?, What am I doing here?, Where did I come from?, When did it all take place?, and Why am I here? The oft-added "H question" would be: How did it all happen? If you substitute the entire universe for the first-person pronoun, you arrive at the most succinct form of posing the questions addressed by stories of creation or, dressed up in the vocabulary of science, cosmogonies—from *kosmos* (world) and *gonia* (to give birth or beget).

Depending on who asks them and the conditions under which they are posed, questions of origin become more specific, more refined: What are we afraid of? Why do we die? Where do we go when we die? Why are there different sexes, races, and languages? Where did those lights in the sky come from? And all that stuff that comes out of the openings in my body? Stories that tell about creation represent one of the earliest human attempts to answer such questions. And the ones that endure—"have legs," as the journalists say—depend a lot on the storyteller.

The Cave of Altamira on the north coast of Spain houses some of the world's most realistic-looking ancient charcoal drawings and polychrome paintings of bison, horses, huge antlered deer, and other animals. The cave walls of Lascaux in the Dordogne region of southwest France add mountain lions and au-

rochs, ancestors of present-day cattle, to the gallery of creatures that lived alongside the people who portrayed them. With
skilled hands and sharp eyes, their makers crafted imagery
equal in aesthetic quality to that of any contemporary artist.
Archaeologists have radiocarbon-dated this exquisite imagery
to at least 20,000 BCE, during the Upper Paleolithic or late
Stone Age, prior to the last Ice Age in Europe. Discovered in
1994, the equally eye-catching paintings of Chauvet Cave in
the south of France may date to ten thousand years earlier (the
Aurignacian Period). In addition to horses, woolly rhinos, big
cats, bears, and more auroch, these cave paintings portray a
partial human figure in the shape of a vulva, an avian-looking
creature (possibly a butterfly), an erupting volcano, handprints,
and what appear to be tally marks—all makings for a great
story, indeed several stories.

Some interpreters think that the artists included in their
paintings not only the animals most likely hunted for food
(like the auroch), but also those creatures they feared, and perhaps needed to kill before they could hunt safely. I speculated
in my introduction to *Star Stories* that these images might have
been part of a ritual that preceded the hunt.[3] Imagine partici-
pants gathered around the fire in front of the cave drawings,
their shadows flickering on the dimly lit walls. Perhaps one of
them donned skin and antlers—dried remains from an earlier
kill—while another hunter, club in hand, confronted him. Did
they believe that acting out the hunt would make it happen?
Other observers point to a series of iconic images that look as
if they were created purely for aesthetic purposes; for example,
an array of horse heads suggests an attempt to study that shape.
Maybe the paintings were executed by a school of artists under
the direction of a master? Or is that narrative spin on prehis-
toric art just a reflection of our desire to feel closer to our early
human ancestors?

With language well developed by that time, I wonder what questions the original artists had, and what stories those questions may have inspired, as they stood in front of the Altamira, Lascaux, or Chauvet paintings. Surely some of the same questions struck those who entered the caves and beheld the magnificent exhibits millennia after the last Ice Age. By then many of the animals pictured on the walls were no longer part of the landscape; they had either moved on to greener pastures or become extinct. Latter-day observers might have wondered: Where did these masterpieces come from? How did they get here? Who made them and what happened to them? What do they mean?—some of the same questions we ask today. For as long as a people share a narrative about what happened in the past—and we all do, even though some scholars insist on lumping people who lived prior to the invention of writing into "traditional," or ahistorical, cultures—they will create and tell stories that change with time to fit the circumstances and the questions foremost in their minds. We know that at least a million years before the cave paintings, people were fabricating tools and jewelry, developing complex burials to care for their dead, and even making drawings. They had all the requisite senses for experiencing, and the skills for representing, the world around them. These skills included the ability to create narratives about what they feared—danger and death—and what they hoped for, that is, sustenance and stability. The first stories of creation must have begun, as so many opening lines of myths do: "Very long ago . . ."

Today most compilers of creation stories work within the discipline of the history of religion.[4] These scholars are concerned principally with similarities and differences among monotheistic and polytheistic systems and with the classification of mythic types.[5] The most widely recognized system encompasses

five kinds of creation myths: creation from nothing (most familiar to us in biblical Genesis); creation from a previously
undifferentiated state (chaos) represented by either primary
elements or a physical birth object such as an egg; creation
from some sort of alteration in a static, primeval state, such as
the union or separation of world parents; creation via emergence, for example from holes in the earth or sky; and finally,
creation via a character or force that dives into the depths of
primordial waters. Though my storytelling will offer a different focus, I intend to address each of these scenarios, or types,
where they apply.

What is it about humankind that compels us to relate the
stories of our lives to the landscape and skyscape? An inquir-
ing anthropologist once asked this question of a young Navajo
girl, who answered, with brilliant simplicity, that we do so to
keep our thoughts in order, to keep things from happening to
us. Anthropologists, or those who focus on culture, also have
occasion to retell creation stories of the people they study. They
usually document these stories, which are inseparable from
the specific locations where they originate, in a detailed and
informative way. But because their work is highly culture specific, anthropologists rarely compare creation narratives across
diverse peoples.

"Myths are original revelations of the pre-conscious psy-
che, involuntary statements about unconscious happenings
and anything but allegories of physical process." So state com-
parative cosmologists of the Jungian psychology school, who
argue that myths find their origin in the collective unconscious,
with all characters and events an expression of archetypes common to all cultures of thinking beings.[6] Thus a common pattern is thought to underlie all myth, with all that we can possibly experience originating in an eternal transcendent source
that fuels a psychic unity in human thought. For example, the

desire for the afterlife and belief in the existence of a magical substance that can be ingested to get there—think of Ponce de León's search for the Fountain of Youth—was already present before people ever experienced particular plants and beverages as a way to communicate with their ancestors. In other words, the pattern is already there and only later gets put into practice when, say, a shaman is influenced by a substance. But maybe we should ask ourselves which was more likely to happen first: the idea of an afterlife consisting of a soul liberated from the restrictions of time and space, or the discovery of hallucinogenic plants that liberate one from ordinary time and space—thus offering those who ingest them ideas of a new and extraordinary experience? Perhaps the Jungian psychologists put the cart before the horse.[7]

In contrast to these established approaches to creation mythology, I will focus on what the storyteller experiences in the landscape.[8] But we must think of landscape not simply as what we see when we look around us—mountains, streams, rivers, buildings, a skyline. Instead it is a composite of land and sky and *people.* In most creation stories you can't separate places from people. The landscape is conceived as a distinct whole, with all its parts functioning together. It is animate—breathing, vibrant, interactive. Careful observers of the world around them designed their creation myths as sensible ways to explain the unfolding of politics, history, social relationships, and ideas about life after death. The most effective storytellers forged lasting links between what happens in the observable world and just about every phase of human activity that mattered to them. Listeners came to understand themselves as mediators in a powerful universal discourse. At stake lay the battle between fate and free will, between body and soul.

This book, then, will take us on a trek across space, time, and culture—both past and present. Along the way, I'll share ways that humans have sought to understand the universe, paying special attention to how both myth and science contribute to our ever-changing understanding of the phenomena that shape our experiences in this world.

INTRODUCTION

Creation Landscapes

In the beginning, God created the heavens and the earth. The
earth was without form and void, and darkness was upon the
face of the deep; and the Spirit of God was moving
over the face of the waters.
And God said, "Let there be light"; and there was light. And God
saw that the light was good; and God separated the light from
the darkness. God called the light Day, and the darkness he
called Night. And there was evening and
there was morning, one day.
And God said, "Let there be a firmament in the midst of the
waters, and let it separate the waters from the waters." And God
made the firmament and separated the waters which were under
the firmament from the waters which were above the firmament.
And it was so.
And God called the firmament Heaven. And there was evening
and there was morning, a second day. And God said, "Let the
waters under the heavens be gathered together into one place,
and let the dry land appear." And it was so.

—Genesis 1:1–9

For many readers, the creation story found in Genesis, the first book of the Bible, is the most familiar.[1] Believed by modern scholars to have been written by multiple authors during the sixth and fifth centuries BCE, it is among a select group of creation stories that form the backbone of the Western tradition.

The word "genesis" means origination, and every genesis myth begins with a sense of time. In this story, you can feel the sense of time like so many heartbeats. Rhythmic pulses offer a sense of the way the story might have been sung or chanted long before the advent of writing: "And God said . . . ; And it was so."

Genesis tells of an orderly creation. *Ex nihilo* (out of nothing)—solely by the power of words—God makes heaven first, then the earth; then day and night are separated out of chaos. Later, God creates vegetation, celestial bodies to mete out the calendar, animals, and, last of all, man:

> And God said, "Let the earth bring forth living creatures according to their kinds: cattle and creeping things and beasts of the earth according to their kinds." And it was so.
>
> And God made the beasts of the earth according to their kinds and the cattle according to their kinds, and everything that creeps upon the ground according to its kind. And God saw that it was good.
>
> Then God said, "Let us make man in our image." (Genesis 1:24–26)

Whoever wrote this Genesis creation story needed to believe in an orderly world, one that is intentional, purposeful, created specifically with humans in mind, and, above all, good.

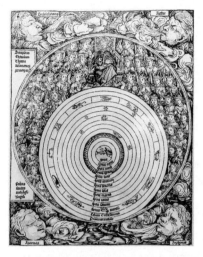 

Picturing the seven days of Genesis. (Hartmann Schedel,
Liber Chronicarium mundi. Left: photo by Heinz-Josef Lücking;
right: Courtesy of the Lessing J. Rosenwald Collection,
Rare Book and Special Collections Division, The Library of
Congress, Washington, DC)

Indeed, Genesis offers little detail about cosmic forces in what
we would call the natural world and focuses more on how to
live the good life, repeating the word "good" frequently in each
of its first nine chapters.

The structure of time in Genesis, then, is paralleled by
spatial order that is also hierarchical, with a sense of right and
wrong, good and bad. If we try to reconstruct a picture to go
with the words, we end up with a stacked, multilayered universe—a testament to the adaptability of an ancient creation
story to a newer age.

Biblical scholars think the Genesis myth of creation was
written after Exodus, which tells of the emergence of a new
people, the Israelites—slaves who survived the defeat of the
Egyptians and were led by their God to settle in a new land.

The natural phenomena that existed in primordial time, and which are featured in most other myths, are not the basic forms through which God, called Yahweh (or Jehovah) in the Old Testament, expresses himself. Instead he is revealed through events in human history, through the order in which creation takes place (dark and watery, daylight, sky, earth, vegetation, celestial bodies, reptiles and birds, other animals, and finally people).

To recognize themselves as a distinct ethnic group, the Israelites chose Yahweh as their patron deity. But what made their creation story unusual and, as judged by historians, so lasting, was the tradition that no other gods should be worshipped. Here was a creation by Yahweh alone—the beginning of monotheism. The reference to "us" in the making of people in Genesis reflects the competing polytheism of creation myths that already existed in the Middle East during the fifth and sixth centuries BCE.

There is in Genesis a second story (2:4–23) that features a more hands-on creation process. Man (specifically Adam) is fashioned out of earth, the source of all life. Like a creator-craftsman, God molds him from a ball of clay into a preexisting environment. Realizing that it would be better if the human race consisted of paired opposites—male and female—rather than single individuals, God creates Eve. The original pair confront evil and struggle to cope with the problems of living under a higher authority—the same problem encountered by the newly created generation of deities in both the Greek *Theogony* and the Babylonian *Enuma Elish* creation stories we'll deal with later. The fall of man surely begins with the first bite of the well-known apple, but—like the tide to which all celestial bodies are subjected—man rises again. He returns from his chaotic origin via a series of acts oriented toward his ultimate salvation.

The second creation story stresses the idea that, though past historical events alternated between harmony and discord, all will lead ultimately to world order. First, God creates an environment of righteousness, harmony, and well-being, replete with a covenant—a promise by man to follow the law He has laid down. The injustice and sin in the world constitute the discord created by man. Each time he breaks the law by sinning, he is called in for judgment. Only an act of divine justice can restore the balance and return man—forgiven and transformed, repentant for his sins—back to orderly society. The stories of Cain and Abel, the temptation of Adam in the Garden of Eden, Noah and the Flood, and the Tower of Babel illustrate this pattern of the rise and fall, the sense of tension followed by the feeling of relaxation. For example, take the sequence in the story of Cain and Abel:

1. Cain falls; he breaks the law by killing his brother out of jealousy.
2. He is called to judgment.
3. Punishment is administered (his land shall no longer be fruitful despite all his hard work).
4. He is restored. God protects him by placing a mark on him.

The sense of cyclical time embedded within these biblical stories, as in many early myths, stands in contrast to the absolute, linear idea of time offered to the contemporary world by geology and astronomy, which measure important periods in millions or billions of years. For the stories, what matters more than duration is the order of events and the harmonic overtones that resonate in the cyclic flow of historical time. The head of time's arrow points to the tail. What happens once, happens again, though things are a little different the second time. Cain falls; Cain is restored; but he is different the next time around.

I think the way we read Exodus offers a lesson in how we ought to respond to all myths of creation, especially in the literal-minded present: don't dismiss the story as worthless if it doesn't make sense to *you*. In the opinion of most biblical scholars, the dramatic story of Exodus is likely based, at least in part, on actual events. Why make up a story that stressed the point of view of a powerless people enslaved in a foreign land unless there's some truth to it? Historical research tells us that Semitic people were among those enslaved in Egypt. No doubt some of them must have escaped and made their way across the Sinai, where they merged with the budding Israelite population to the north. Conflating and retelling such stories likely gave rise to the epic narrative we read in the Old Testament. It is, after all, the story and meanings that become attached to it that matter as much as the facts of history. And the food of mythic knowledge is never pure fiction.[2]

Though both Genesis and Exodus offer little detail about cosmic forces in what we would call the natural world, the Exodus route does refer to a distinct natural environment. Yam Suph (Sea of reeds), the Red Sea, is a likely reference to the Gulf of Suez. There, as one tradition has it, Yahweh casts Pharaoh and his army into the sea's depths. In another account—the one favored by Hollywood—Moses parts the sea with a strong wind, turning it into dry land, which allows the Israelites to cross unharmed, then, when the sea returns to its normal depth, it inundates the pursuing oppressors. Is there a rational explanation for what actually took place? Were there extreme tides that could have helped the Israelites in their time of need? Perhaps the Egyptians were done in by a lucky tidal wave? Some scientists have devised a set of mathematical equations to study wind-induced wave motion in a shallow sea. One study concluded that a sustained twenty-four-hour wind averaging 110 kilometers (67 mi.) an hour would have been sufficient to blow most of the water out of the shallow lower reef in the northern part of the Gulf of Suez.[3] The fleeing Israelites could then have made the crossing on foot in about four hours before the water returned to its normal level. Science finds a clever way to avoid a miracle! But a miracle is what happens when a story meets people who are prepared to receive it as a miracle, wrote theologian Martin Buber.[4] Whatever happened, what's most important is how the people *interpreted* what happened. And as it turned out, the story of the Israelites' journey out of Egypt would become an abiding pillar in their identity. Exodus had legs.

First the heavens, then the earth, veggies, birds and animals, and, last of all, people to manage and care for this new earthly home—all fashioned out of chaos via the spoken word of a single supreme deity. It may be familiar, but this story board is not the basis for all possible creation scripts. A story told by the Inuit of far northern Canada, for example, opens with undifferentiated animals and people, all talking to one another and looking the same. In the Ainu creation story from Japan, the world is created on the back of a preexisting fish; in the Samoan, it comes from a split rock, or a brother-sister pair with oversized sexual organs who roamed the empty universe in Aboriginal Australian Dreamtime. In other stories, instead of words issuing from the mouth, the power of creation emanates from other bodily orifices—semen from the genitals of the Egyptian creator Atum, or fecal matter from the anus of the Raven god of the Haida. The Bantu say their god Boshongo vomited up the universe.

Chaos—the stuff of creation—takes on various forms too. It can range from nothing at all (Swahili) to the bodily parts of the creator him- or herself (Babylonian, Norse, and Amazonian). It can be bits of mud hauled up from below (Haudenosaunee, sometimes called Iroquois) or sand and stones dropped down from above (Kayan, from Borneo). Some creator deities look almost comical, especially when you compare them with their Judeo-Christian patriarchal counterpart. Take the trickster Raven deities of northwest U.S. and Canadian coastal tribal cultures, and the Nez Perce Coyote. Both creatures are noted for their humorous discoveries of first foods: Raven discovers berries and salmon while hiding out in a clam shell, and Coyote tricks a monster into letting him enter his stomach to search for friends (a deliciously satisfying outcome for Coyote).

Creation from a cosmic egg is featured in stories from cultures as far apart as the Dyak of Borneo, who say that two primeval water birds laid a pair of eggs that hatched to form the sky and the earth, and the Dogon of Africa: they tell of a giant stirring in the universe that cracked open a cosmic egg deposited by the Supreme Being, which then gave birth to all things. And in the Finnish *Kalevala* epic, the Mother of the Waters, a bird deity, lays eggs that fall into the sea and break open, creating the land, sun, moon, and stars. It seems that more than one early version of our modern Big Bang Theory begins with an egg.[5]

Some creator deities come in pairs, mother and father for example. Family generational problems lie at the root of many world parent-creation myths, which usually open with an eternal union that must be broken apart—usually by the children—in order for creation to take place. Some stories begin with attempts by the offspring to separate their parents—the sky and the earth, or the salty and sweet water—by physically prying them apart. A cosmic battle of the personified forces of nature highlights the action in many of these tales; for example, fire versus ice in the Norse creation story. The *Enuma Elish* and the

Greek *Theogony* are also good examples—so is the Polynesian heaven and earth story. In each, the dismembered body of one of the parents becomes the orderly universe we observe today.

The most imaginative storytellers describe shape shifts and other drastic transformations of multiple characters affecting the creation process. Metamorphosis dominates the narrative of the creation story of the Dobu Islanders of the Western Pacific. Fire from an old woman's pubes turns into the first humans, who continually change into trees and yams—then back again. Resolving the chicken-egg problem in cyclic time, some humans metamorphose into birds who lay eggs out of which humans hatch. In the Babylonian story, the body of the motherly parent changes in two ways: the stomach is transformed into the sun's path, while her blood and bones become humans. And while the bones of the dismembered Norse god of the frozen north are turned into mountains, his teeth and jaws morph into rocks and stones, and his skull becomes the sky.

The transformations described in these stories are clearly prompted by careful observations of changes in the visible world. Erupting volcanoes rise up out of the sea, islands and coasts are submerged by flood, streams and rivers silt up along their sinuous courses, deer grow and shed antlers, and caterpillars miraculously turn into butterflies. The more attention you pay to what goes on in the world around you, the more you realize how many surprising changes are taking place.

Along with separation and transformation, emergence is a central process in many stories of creation. We witness it in worms and termites that spring from the ground and maggots from decayed flesh. Excreta issue from every organ of the body. Most unforgettable of all for those fortunate enough to witness it, an offspring (an apt word) appears out of the womb of its mother.

It's no surprise, therefore, that after the earth-diver gods descend through sky holes, Navajo people emerge from holes in
the earth. In the world of the Inuit, animals poke their heads
out of holes in the snow as if they had originated from seeds
planted there. In Iroquois creation, a turtle is summoned to
dive to the bottom of the waters below and bring up a handful
of mud, creating Turtle Island, which eventually grows to the
size of the North American continent. In the Siberian Buryat
myth, the diver is a water bird, in the Altaic version a goose,
in one Mongolian variant, a loon, a masterful diver that can
stay underwater for a mysteriously long time.

Our modern scientific version of genesis began some fourteen
billion years ago in a colossal explosion out of which all events
and things emerged. Usually implicit in every genesis is a purpose, though for many of us the "why?" of that original cataclysmic event seems elusive. As Nobel laureate Steven Weinberg
famously put it: "The more the universe seems comprehensi-
ble, the more it also seems pointless. There is no solace in the
fruits of our research."[6] The stories presented here celebrate
the creative fearlessness of humans who have invented a narrative path out of such incomprehensibility and despair. But
how can we begin to organize and contrast such inventive and
inspired creation stories from across the world? We could ar-
range them by theme, or bring together myths told in the various kinds of cultures and civilizations: hunter-gatherer, agrarian, city-state, kingdom, or empire.[7] But I have chosen to pay
special attention to the observation of nature—how the imagination of the teller takes what is seen and otherwise sensed in
the landscape and weaves a lasting narrative that addresses the
big questions that animate so much of human culture. Though
I will point out common themes—creation by word, world parents, emerging earth divers, and others—I will focus on how

each story is rooted firmly in things observed in the physical, biological, geological, and celestial environments shared by narrator and listener.

Mountains and caves may be the most obvious landscape settings for creation stories. They represent the entrances to heaven and the underworld, respectively, in many world cosmologies that conceive of the universe in stacked vertical layers—heaven above, the underworld below, and the place inhabited by people in between—often connected together by a world axis.[8] The water that enters the earth's surface both from above, in the form of rain, and below, via springs and artesian wells, offers another stage for creation. A unique landscape also presents itself in the midst of the three-quarters of the earth's surface covered by water. People who live in island environments offer a variety of answers to their creation questions based on what they sense in their landscapes, as do those who live in ice- and snow-bound lands at the frigid extremities of the world.

I begin with stories originating in mountainous places— from Mount Olympus, home of the Greek gods, to the western mountains of North and South America, where vertical pillars support the sky and creator deities symbolizing the earthquake, volcano, and landslide chase one another over a treacherous up and down terrain, turning one another into prominent geological formations. The riverine dwellers we encounter next tell of a creation out of mounds of silt deposited along riverbanks during flood season and in the chaotic, foggy territory where they empty into the ocean. In West Africa, the carcass of the deity out of which all was created becomes the great river itself. The karst topographies of Yucatán and South Australia are honeycombed with caves. In these places the action shifts to entrances to the underworld, where creative forces compete to determine how the world shall come to be. Descendants of the Inca of Peru tell a story of their first king emerging from a cave near the capital of their empire. Creation myths from island habitats will include stories from Polynesia to Indonesia to Japan. Was it all dredged up from below or thrown down from above? Places with extreme meteorological conditions, especially in the high latitudes of the Northern Hemisphere, center around the behavior of snow and ice: a Norse deity emerges from a frozen state; Inuit animals pop up from holes in the snow; and, in the far south, oceans clash at the horn of South America.

I close with a fifth-century BCE Greek creation myth that is striking in the way it is told and the actions and processes it evokes, especially when placed alongside contemporary accounts that address the big questions—like the Big Bang and evolution by adaptation. But don't be surprised when I show how history certifies that this particular myth is the parent of today's scientific stories of creation.

PART ONE

MOUNTAINS

If some creation myths are to be believed, mountains are the closest thing humans have to heaven on earth. That may be why the ancient Greeks chose Mount Olympus—which they called the threshold of heaven—as their ideal place to locate their gods to keep them close. We begin there with the *Theogony,* a 2,700-year-old tale that takes place in the northern Peloponnese. The story opens with a father's jealousy over the attention given his children by his mate. (The gods seem to behave just like the people at the foot of the mountain who tell their stories.)

Next we journey to the Himalayas, where two kinds of energy—earth and sky—born of a primeval egg, become separated in a universe that expands on a vast time scale. Sound familiar? In the ensuing battle, a rip in the sky results in a tilted landscape. Have a look at a topographic map of China and you'll see the result of the hasty mending process.

Traveling down the mountainous spine of the two American continents, we explore creation stories told by a variety of montane inhabitants. The Navajo believe that when they see a particular mountain, its name evokes a special story that has moral significance. They say that the land makes people live right. In Monument Valley, the red-sandstone region of the southwest United States noted for its towering buttes, the mountains really do seem to support the sky. The action takes place on a four-part stage marked out by sky, mountain—even color directions. As in the *Theogony,* time oscillates rhythmically between order and disorder. The narrative focuses on an age-old social question: Where do our frailties originate, and how can we overcome them? Helping to answer it is the trickster animal who thrives in the Navajo borderlands—the Coyote.

In 1985, on the high plateau in the Sierra Madres called the Valley of Mexico, an 8.0 magnitude earthquake struck Mexico City, killing more than five thousand people and causing four billion dollars in damage. Each year on the September 19 anniversary of the tragedy, survivors are reminded of the smell of death. One of the so-called earthquake's children, a young man born on that fatal morning, recalled: "I was once told that the Earth was so angry I was born, that it chose to kill people." This recent story feels like an echo of an event fifteen hundred years earlier, when, it is told, the nearby ancient city of Cuicuilco was inundated after fire deities emerged out of the earth in the eruption of the Xitle volcano. No written records of the horror experienced by its citizens has survived, but contemporary residents of the valley are mindful of the ever-present threat of Popocatépetl, whose smoking cinder cone looms above the southeast horizon. Transforming what they feared most in their natural surroundings into their ultimate source of power, the mighty Aztecs drew on the mighty environmental forces of earthquake and fire, in addition to wind and flood, to tell their story of "The Five Suns of Creation."

From the sharply vertical slopes between the Andean highlands and the Pacific coast of South America comes a story of how the powers of fire and water compete in a series of contests to decide the fate of the world. The actions of these gods of nature parallel the concerns of the people who spar over the control of water, which in some places drops 4,500 meters (15,000 ft.) to the sea over a mere 160 kilometers (100 mi.).

Finally, we descend to the sacred landscape of the Andean foothills of western Amazonia, where the gods of the Southern Arawak people, like the deities of their highland ancestors, have a habit of transforming those they disagree with into stone. The creation story recounted by the Southern Arawak paints a mental map of their origin—a common narrative form in tales of beginnings told by migratory people. Like those of their ancestors from the highlands, the gods exhibit a habit of transforming people they disagree with into stone.

1

Power Politics on Mount Olympus

Compared to Genesis, Hesiod's *Theogony*—literally, "genealogy of the gods"—from the eighth century BCE, sounds like an X-rated fairy tale rife with family feuds. The action takes place on Mount Olympus, home of the gods, a spectacularly steep mountain range in northern Greece consisting of more than fifty dramatic peaks that rise up sharply to nearly 3,000 meters (10,000 ft.). For the Greeks, Mount Olympus was a threshold where heaven seemed to meet the earth, and so seemed a natural place for deities to live, close to the people who worshipped them.[1]

The ancient Greeks also said that the Hyperboreans, a race of giants who resided beyond the north wind, perhaps on the other side of heaven, worshipped these same deities. Theirs was a perfect land, and its inhabitants lived in complete happiness there for a thousand years, thanks in part to their devotion to Apollo, the sun god, who elected to spend the winter among them shining brightly both day and night.

Hyperborea, literally "beyond the North Wind" (Boreas), was thought to be a continent located north of Thrace and

Mount Olympus, home of the gods. (Edward Lear, *Mount Olympus from Larissa, Thessaly, Greece,* 1850–1885. Gift of Estate of Florence B. Selden, in memory of Carl L. Selden, 1996, Metropolitan Museum of Art, New York, 1996.205)

bordered by the great river-ocean that circled the world. There, sealed off from the Greek world by impassable snow-covered mountains, a benevolent race of giants thrived in eternal spring-time. But why imagine a warm climate so far north? Anyone familiar with the increase in the noontime altitude of the sun is aware of its northern advance as summer approaches, bring-ing with it more daylight hours. From such observations it would be easy to extrapolate to envision a place that experi-ences continuous daylight—the land of the midnight sun. Arc-tic dwellers pay the price for months of continuous daytime in summer by experiencing an equally lengthy period of dark-ness in winter. Notwithstanding, the legend of the utopian Hyperborean climate would later lead to the widespread be-lief, still evident in the romantic imagination of the eighteenth century, that an open water route leading to the North Pole would reveal a habitable paradise in an ice-free sea.

Reading *Theogony* tells us a lot about how the Greeks thought about time as well as space. Events in the narrative seem to oscillate back and forth, like a pendulum from one extreme to the other, between activity and inactivity. First, order is taken for granted; next there is a threat to that order; then order is reestablished; and so on, in perpetuity.[2]

Our storyteller is the Greek poet Hesiod, second only in fame to Homer. Hesiod was a hard-bitten farmer who lived around 700 BCE. In addition to the high-minded *Theogony*, he wrote *Works and Days*, which addresses mundane issues in his workaday life, such as time management connected to the hard labor involved in maintaining the farm, and the difficulty of finding justice in life. In *Works and Days*, in which Hesiod elaborates on the "five ages (races) of man" and the common origin of men and gods, he comes off as a natural grumbler and pessimist, frequently complaining about his struggle to eke out a living from the rock-laden, thin soil of the Peloponnese. His more exalted *Theogony* appears during a time of Greek awakening from hard times. Following the fall of the Mycenaean kingdoms three centuries earlier, minor aristocratic lords had risen up to hold power in fragmented city-state units.[3] Now the culture was expansive, with the Greek people colonizing the Mediterranean, developing written literature, and building great temples. And it was outward looking, possessing enough leisure of thought to address ultimate questions, like, Where did we come from?

The *Theogony* is all about power—how the powers of the gods came to be organized. As in other succession myths we'll encounter (for example, the Babylonian *Enuma Elish*, which likely influenced it), the story revolves around a battle of the generations. The history of the world is portrayed as a story of how Zeus inherited his rule from his godly predecessors.

Time did not begin until Gaia (the earth) and Ouranos (the sky) lay together. But Gaia (just like a woman, in storyteller

Hesiod's eyes) was sexually promiscuous, unpredictable, and incestuous. Her son Ouranos already had been born out of his mother's affair with Erebus—darkness personified—who, like the Night and Gaia herself, had arisen out of Chaos, the first power—that indiscernible, dark abyss of many mixed qualities churning around in a disorderly state.

Mother Earth's labor was made difficult by Father Sky's jealousy and outright fear of each of his prospective offspring. He attempted to relieve his stress by "unbirthing" them—literally shoving his children back into the womb as they were being born. Mother Earth dealt with this irritating situation by fashioning a secret weapon:

> So he hid them away, each one, as they came into being,
> and let them not rise to the light from down in the
>   hollow of the earth. . . .
> But huge Gaia was groaning within and feeling
>   constrained,
> and so she contrived an evil device.
> Swiftly producing a new kind of metal, gray adamant,
> she created of it a great sickle, and this she displayed to
> her children.[4]

Next-born Kronos, Father Time himself, used his famous sickle to sever his father's male member. He tossed it into the sea, where its shining foam gave birth to the female deity Aphrodite, goddess of love.

A curious ritual associated with Kronos later developed into a sort of new year's celebration in which masters and slaves reversed roles. The Greeks often spoke of an age that might follow that of Zeus: a time when men would be born from their graves and grow younger, when all the strife inflicted on the world would shrivel and disappear, when time would literally reverse itself and flow backward. But what is it about Kronos that makes him an appropriate symbol for Father Time? Like the swing of a pendulum—or the times of our lives alternating cyclically between good and bad—what he represents is depicted by a series of actions that go back and forth between extremes: one action seems to be the reverse of the other, in contrast to our modern notion of time as an endless linear chain of events. Kronos castrates his father for pushing children back into his mother's womb. Later he swallows his own children, but when Zeus overthrows him, he is induced to regurgitate their essence again. Kronos is aptly named.

Today we still associate Kronos, as Old Father Time, with the new year, a time at the end of our seasonal cycle when we resolve to make drastic changes to better ourselves, even if those resolutions often fail. In later Hellenic times, ringing in the new year took on an agrarian symbolism. The act of castration mentioned in *Theogony* can be thought to symbolize the annual cutting of the seed from the stalk, which enables Mother Earth to become fruitful and bear a bounteous harvest. The reversal of roles experienced at year's end—think of the replacement of Old Father Time by a newborn baby, or associating the beginning of life with the onset of death in the form of the grim reaper—mirrors the way things in nature really do appear to reverse themselves at the extreme point of time's seasonal oscillation. For just as a pendulum reverses its direction, so does the place where the sun rises and sets glide on its annual course back and forth along the horizon, while the moon passes forward and backward, revealing its facial aspects through its phases.

As the warming sun, which had climbed ever higher in the sky to nourish the earth, descends its celestial ladder once again, a succession of polar opposites transpires in the world beneath it. The dramatic reversal of behavior of plants and animals at the peak time of their life cycle is obvious to anyone who pays attention to the environment. Just after the fruit is born, the leaves on the trees shrivel and drop off: they literally "ungrow"—become "unborn" again. Animals burrow back into their holes whence they had come in the spring. Hesiod and others of his era surely sensed these seasonal reversals taking place in the agrarian environment, because their lives depended on them.

The Greeks believed that Kronos created this pattern of opposites when, out of the symmetry of chaos, he polarized the universe. He fabricated time when he parted the earth and the sky, and he separated the male principal that fell into the sea to become its own opposite, the female essence in the form of Aphrodite. Thus Kronos created that mobile element of becoming that causes things to oscillate between the two extremes of our worldly existence—time.

Continuing with the story, *Theogony* descends into a lengthy genealogical catalogue of alternating good and evil deities who represent different parts and powers of a highly animate, personified universe. Like the developing Greek state, this imagined cosmos consists of both political and natural components. Zeus, king of the gods and bringer of all order to the world of mortals, becomes its end product. Unlike his siblings, Zeus had been hidden away by his mother, who duped her husband into swallowing a stone instead. Ouranos was forced to regurgitate the stone, which ultimately ended up on Mount Olympus, where it became an altar intended for the worship of Zeus. Reared and nurtured in secrecy, the future king of the gods was able to return to complete the conquest of his father. But opposing forces, seeking to avenge Ouranos's death, sent forth the monster Typhoeus—the storm that comes from the sea (whence our word "typhoon")—the youngest of Gaia's children and hideous beyond all description:

Wonderfully strong were the arms of Typhoeus
to do all he wanted;
he had the weariless feet of a mighty divinity; and out
of his
shoulders a hundred heads of a serpent, a frightening
dragon,
rose, each of which shot forth a flickering black tongue;
and out of his
eyes flashed fire from under the brows of each of his
heads,
fire came blazing forth from each of his staring heads;
and from each of his terrible heads he was able to speak
and
utter every imaginable sound.[5]

Now to battle: Zeus summoned up his strength, grabbed
his weapons, and, in a violent episode capable of riveting ancient listeners' attention as much as any big-screen action-hero
scene would today:

did he, swooping down from Olympos, strike him and
burn off all the marvelous heads of that very frightening monster.
And he, being subdued with lashing blow upon blow,
fell on his knees in defeat,
and huge Gaia groaned in response.
Fire spurted out of that god, that thunder-bolted
divinity,
when he was struck in the glens of the mountain, the
rocky Aidna, into submission.[6]

Once order had been established in heaven, Kronos set
out to create the Races of Man. First came the Golden Race.

They lived like the gods under the reign of Kronos, peacefully, never aging, never wanting for sustenance—a utopian dream of paradisiacal happiness. But as injustice and hubris entered the world, life degenerated. Zeus hid his father's failed creation in the ground; there the Golden Race lives on as spirits and guardians of the land. In their place Zeus created the Silver Race. Their children were raised at home for a hundred years and lived only brief lives thereafter. But Zeus's creation was scarcely more successful than his father's. His people couldn't control themselves. They injured one another. Worst of all, they didn't have the capacity to worship their gods and make sacrifices to them as a way of recognizing and reciprocating the gift of being brought into the world. So Zeus hid them deeper still in the earth, where they became the spirits of the underworld. Next he made a third race, the Bronze. But in some ways they behaved even worse than their predecessors. Though strong, they were hard-hearted men, lovers of violence and war, and so unruly that they died by their own hands—with bronze weaponry. Ultimately Zeus confined them to the lowest reaches of Hades. Next Zeus managed to break the negative chain of descent by producing a demigod Race of Heroes—the Mycenaean kings, the only race not named after a metal. Once their work was done, Zeus released them and they went to live beyond the ocean that surrounds the world.

Finally Zeus created the fifth race—the Race of Iron—our own. The men of this age needed to work unceasingly, and for some there were too many burdens mixed in with too little good. "Would that I now were no longer alive in the fifth age of men, but had died earlier or had been born at a later time," laments the pessimistic farmer-storyteller Hesiod.[7] Justice is doomed to break down completely. Born later? Did our storyteller anticipate the creation of a new and more exalted race?

2

How China Got Its
Tilted Landscape

The east Asian landscape is diverse and decidedly slanted. In the west lies the Tibetan plateau, which sits an average of 4,500 meters (15,000 ft.) above sea level and is ringed by the high Himalayas to the south and west. To the northwest lie the Taklamakan and Gobi deserts, which reach altitudes of 1,500 meters (5,000 ft.), their sand dunes continually sculpted by the shifting winds. The Gobi is bordered on the east by the active volcanoes of today's Jilin and Heilongjiang provinces. Together the mountains and desert form a barrier that long isolated China from the west. Its three major rivers, the Yellow, Yangtze, and Pearl, descend eastward more than 1,500 kilometers (900 mi.) to the Yellow and China seas, passing through deep chasms in karst mountainous terrain covered by green forests that are home to thousands of species of wild animals.

The myth of Pan Gu (the first living being and creator of all), from southern China, dates from the third century CE. As in other creation stories we'll encounter (from the Norse Ymir or Babylonian Tiamat cultures, for example), the world is created out of the body parts of a sacrificed god. In this case, two kinds of energy burst out of a primeval egg and separate to create an expanding universe on a vast time scale—a scenario thought to bear a tantalizing likeness to the hypothesis of the primeval atom, which would later come to be known as the Big Bang theory of creation.[1]

They say that long ago there was nothing in the universe—only an enormous egg. Inside two forces were scrambled together: the murky, opaque Yin, and the limpid, transparent Yang. Over a long period—some say it took 6,570,000 days (18,000 years)—these energies and substances came into balance, and out of the mix there appeared a hairy, two-horned, two-tusked giant named Pan Gu. The giant opened his eyes and saw only darkness. He listened with his ears and heard only silence. He conjured up a magical ax and swung—landing a mighty chop on the shell of the egg, which divided in two with an ear-splitting crack. Slowly the Yin and the Yang began to separate. All that was dark and heavy sank down and formed the earth, while all that was light and clear floated upward and became the heavens. But would the two halves of the newly created universe come back together? Pan Gu stood anxiously between them and held them apart. As each day passed, the earth thickened by three meters (ten feet) and the sky rose another three meters above him. Pan Gu needed to grow himself to keep up with the expansion.

The giant toiled for another 6,570,000 days, until he felt sure that things were securely held in place, and let loose his grip. Exhausted from his long labors to create the world, Pan Gu then lay down and died. Suddenly a miraculous transformation happened. Pan Gu's last breath turned into wind and clouds, his voice became thunder, his left eye turned into the sun, his right eye the moon. Pan Gu's hair and beard were trans-

The First Being, Pan Gu, who chiseled the sky out of rock.
(C. Williams, *Outlines of Chinese Symbolism and Art Motives*
[Shanghai, 1941])

formed into the stars of the Milky Way, his arms and legs became the tall mountains of the west, and the blood that once
flowed through his veins was changed into the water that would
course thereafter in China's mighty rivers. Pan Gu's teeth and
nails became precious gems and minerals, his bone marrow
diamonds, the fine hairs on his skin vegetation, his muscles
the fertile land, the fleas on his fur the wild animals, and the
sweat from all his hard work the rainwater that would nurture
the world. Born out of a cosmic egg, Pan Gu is now nowhere,
yet he is everywhere—for he gave his life and offered his body
to make the world.

Long after Pan Gu created the world, the serpent-tailed

goddess Nu Wa would make the trees and flowers, the birds and tame animals; but she felt the need to create someone with whom to share it all. So Nu Wa knelt down in the mud by the sea and molded a figure resembling herself, except she gave it legs instead of a long tail like her own. She breathed into the figure to give it life. Nu Wa was very pleased with the way her sculpture turned out, so she made another like it, and another, and another—a host of men and women. They all sang and danced, giving thanks to their creator.

But there were other gods in the world who were not as peace-loving as Nu Wa, and they set about destroying the world Pan Gu had created. There was Gong Gong, the water god, and Zhu Rong, god of fire. They constantly argued over who was more important and when these powerful deities fought, the earth cringed in fear. Earthquakes shook the world; tidal waves and tsunamis flooded it. Volcanoes exploded and set the land afire. The violent pair took their battles up to the heavens, where thunder sounded and lightning flashed. Gong Gong banged his head against Mount Buzhou, one of the eight pillars that held up the sky.[2] Then all four pillars began to crumble and the sky was torn open. Half of it fell down and the earth's axis tilted to the southeast, while what was left of the sky rose to the northwest. Then all the water began to drain from the northwest to the southeast.

Next Gong Gong and Zhu Rong unleashed monsters of their own on the world—dragons and snakes and huge birds. The frightened humans appealed to Nu Wa to save them from total destruction. Just as she had used her hands to create the first humans, Nu Wa set to work. To repair the tear in the sky, she gathered many different colored stones. She melted them in the wildfires, flew up with them, and used them to patch the sky back together. Then she turned to the crumbling pillars. She searched for the biggest turtle she could find and asked him to help out. He agreed and swam down to the bottom of the sea. He turned himself upside down and thrust out his leg to hold up the sky. Nu Wa put out all the fires by gathering up the ashes to smother the flames, and she piled together reeds and pebbles to stop the surging waters. Next she turned her attention to the monsters, for she knew there would be no peace in the world with them constantly swooping down. She reached out her hand and grabbed one of the biggest dragons by the tail, twirling it around faster and faster. All the other monsters looked on in wonder, thinking to themselves: if this is what a goddess can do, there's no way we can fight her and expect to win. So they slunk off and hid themselves, vowing never again to disturb the humans. Meanwhile Zhu Rong and Gong Gong, who had been watching Nu Wa in amazement, realized that her power of creation must be stronger than their combined forces of destruction, so they ceased fighting. Like Pan Gu, Nu Wa, drained from her labors, lay down on the ground and her body became the huge mountain range in the west.

This is how the world returned to peace and beauty. The people rejoiced over the goddess who had given them life. They will never forget what Nu Wa did for the world, thanks to her leaving one trace—a single reminder of the work she had performed with her hands: When she mended the heavens, they remained slightly tilted to the northwest because of the damage done by Gong Gong. That's why the sun, moon, and stars move along daily paths toward the west centered on the Pole Star of the north. They say this is also why the western region of China remained higher than the east, and its rivers still flow toward the south and east.

3

The Four Sides of the
Navajo Universe

On a clear night, head out to a wide-open field and look up at a pitch-black sky studded with stars. Stare at the stars for ten or fifteen minutes. Notice anything? For Northern Hemisphere observers, stars in the east will glide slowly upward and off to the right, while stars in the west will slip downward toward the right at about the same angle to the horizon. Turn and face north, and you'll confront a very different kind of motion. There stars circumnavigate the immovable North Star, moving counter-clockwise round and round a fixed point in the sky, like the tips of so many hands on a clock. Finally, orient to the south and you'll see an imitation of what you saw in the north. Again the stars move round and round, except their trails are clockwise and seem to pivot on a point that lies below the horizon. Regardless of where you are in the world, when it comes to celestial movement, east is the mirror-image of west, while south complements north. Nature seems to be telling us that we live in a four-directional world.

In societies where sky watching mattered, the four directions offered a template when it came to designing a place to live. Navajo elders say that the first home place, the hogan of creation (*ho[o]*, "place," and *ghan*, "home"), was constructed at the edge of the world, where the creator gods emerged. It was in that hogan that the First People made the stars and placed them in the sky. And so, out of reverence to the creator deities, all earthly hogans must be oriented according to the way things move across the night sky. The roof of the household must be peaked or domed like the sky, and it must be round like the shape of the sun, or *ha'a'aah* (the round object that moves in regular fashion), the source of light and heat. Above all, the hogan must face east, the direction in which the sun rises.[1]

Every hogan has four posts, one positioned in each of the cardinal directions, each mimicking one of the four mountains that hold up the sky. The walls of the hogan are vertical—just like the mountains. When you enter you should move clockwise, imitating the sun's motion. The interior is not physically divided, though four specialized areas or recesses—north, east, south, and west—are recognized, along with a fifth direction, the center, which symbolizes the sky that surrounds the central fireplace, the sun. As one elder tells us:

> The hogan is . . . the shelter of the people of the earth, a protection, a home, and a refuge. Because of the harmony in which the hogan is built, the family can be together to endure hardships and grow as a part of the harmony between the sacred mountains, under the care of "Mother Earth" and "Father Sky."[2]

The prominence of directional mountains becomes obvious to anyone who visits Monument Valley, a red-sand desert region on the U.S. Arizona-Utah border in the Navajo home-

The Pillars of Creation: Monument Valley, Navajo Territory,
U.S. Southwest. (Illustration by Pat Aveni)

land. The area is known for its towering lifelike sandstone
buttes; for example, from Merrick Butte looking north, the
West and East Mitten Buttes resemble two gigantic mittens
with inward facing thumbs, their flat tops holding up the sky.

Diné Bahane' (Telling about the people) is the colorful
action myth of Navajo creation. Filled with the same sort of
generational and gender conflict themes found in other stories
of beginnings, it stresses the human desire to seek harmony
and balance with the forces of nature. The core of the Navajo
narrative is an adventure story about cycles of emergence by
people from one world into the next through holes in layers
of a vertically arranged universe.[3] Action heroes ascend and
descend through layers of existence to which only they can
bring order and meaning by gradually transforming the unfa-
miliar to the familiar. The harmony they seek can be achieved

and maintained only through repetitive human-animal action and interaction.

The story opens with a description of their four-part universe. There are four streams that flow outward from the center, in the cardinal directions toward a surrounding ocean. Different races dwell in each quarter, each designated by a color: white in the east like the dawn, blue in the south like the day, yellow in the west like the twilight, and black in the north like the night.

Of a time long, long ago these things are said.

> It is said that at *Tó bil dahisk'id* white arose in the east and was considered day. We now call that spot Place Where the Waters Crossed.
>
> Blue arose in the south. It too was considered day. So the *Nilch'i dineʼé*, who already lived there, moved around. We would call them Air-Spirit People in the language spoken today by those who are given the name *Bilagáana*, which means White Man.
>
> In the west yellow arose and showed that evening had come. Then in the north black arose.... [These] Air-Spirit People are people unlike the five-fingered Earth-Surface People who come into the world today.... [They] live on the ground for a while, die at a ripe old age, and then leave the world. They are people who travel in the air and fly swiftly like the wind and dwell nowhere else but here.[4]

But some of these insect-like people who lived in the four quarters of the First World, especially the Air-Spirit People of the south, fought among themselves. They committed adultery, saying they couldn't help it. The inhabitants of the other quarters were offended by this behavior and told the Air-Spirit

People to find some other place to live. Said the others: "We do not want you here."[5] And so these Air-Spirit People left their familiar world. They traveled upward across the dome of the sky for a long time. Finally they encountered a hole in the sky near the eastern horizon. When they entered it they emerged into a Second World, the land of the blue-headed Swallow People who resided in blue houses on a large flat blue plain.

At first the intruders were treated with suspicion. Exclaimed the leader of the Swallows to the immigrants from the world below:

> "Until you arrived here, no one besides us has ever lived in this world. We are the only ones living here."
>
> The newcomers then had this suggestion to make to the swallows:
> "You are like us in many ways," they suggested.
> "You understand our language."
> "Like us you have legs; like us you have bodies; like us you have wings; like us you have heads."
> "Why can't we become friends?"
> Then the swallows:
> "Let it be as you say," they replied.
> "You are welcome here among us."[6]

So it was that the two sets of people began to treat each other as members of one tribe. They mingled one among the others and called each other by familiar names. They called each other grandparent and grandchild, brother and sister; they called each other father and son, mother and daughter.

At least for a while the two races lived together in harmony, until one of the insect males became a bit too friendly with the Swallow chief's wife. The chief confronted the Air-

Spirit People and lectured them: "We treated you as friends and as kin. And this is how you return our kindness! Well you must leave this world, too; we will have you here no longer."[7]

Banished once again, the Air-Spirit People traveled upward to the top of the Second World's sky. They found an opening at the southern horizon. There they entered a Third World, a yellow-colored domain inhabited by Grasshopper People. But before too long the intruders wronged the chief by violating social customs, and the wandering Air-Spirit People were forced once more to take flight. They flew to the top of the Third World, where they encountered yet another sky; there they chanced to enter another world through a hole at its western horizon. This time they were confronted by an even stranger Fourth World—a world of changing colors that alternated between white, blue, yellow, and black. But nobody seemed to live there and there was no sun or moon to light the sky, just a snow-covered peak in each direction. After many days of searching the strange new land the Insect People finally encountered a race of people stranger than any they ever could have imagined. These people cut their hair; they groomed themselves; they married; they cultivated the land and they offered their visitors corn and squash to eat. The denizens of the First and Fourth Worlds got to know one another. As a result the insect people learned to cleanse themselves, to mind their ways.

One day when the Insect People were bathing and the women were drying themselves with yellow corn meal and the men with white corn meal, they were magically transformed into First Man and First Woman. Nevertheless, like real people they were tempted to commit incest and to quarrel, but this time the Insect People had enough sense to seek a new path on their own. So in the Fourth World harmony began to overcome disorder. After a lengthy series of adventures they managed to find their way through one more aperture—the one that led to the Fifth World, the world we know today. This is where they finally could live in total harmony with one another and with nature.

Now First Man and First Woman needed to illuminate their Fifth World. They chiseled an object in the shape of a dish out of rock crystal. They arranged bits of turquoise around the edge of this dish that became the sun. Outside it they placed rays of red rain. Beyond that they placed bars of lightning. Next they fashioned the moon in the same shape as the sun. They made it out of rock-star mica. To adjust and refine the cosmos to suit the people's needs, they also created the months with their cycle of moon phases.

But where should the sun appear to make the dawn? The east wind persuaded them to bring the new light to his horizon, where sacred soil from the Fourth World below had been spread. The moon was carried to the same region. They say that when you die you will be placed in the care of sun and moon as fair exchange for the work you do here in the Fifth World. But the nighttime sky of the Fifth World was still too dark, especially for travelers who went out when there was no moon. And so First Man and First Woman took little bits of shiny rock-star mica and molded them into millions of stars.

Then First Man sketched out a plan for arranging the stars in the heavens into constellations. He placed one star in the north at a place where it would never move, so that nighttime travelers could fix the direction of their course by it. Close by to help locate it he placed seven more pieces of rock-star mica—the seven stars of the Big Dipper. Next he placed a bright cluster of mica in the west and another in the sky to the east—Evening and Morning Star. This was the way that First Man slowly built the constellations we see today. He worked like a skilled craftsperson to make the results of his work perfect.

Now First Man and First Woman set about embellishing the surface of their new habitat by naming mountains: In the east they made Sisnaajiní, or Sierra Blanca Peak. In the south they made Tsoodzil, or Mount Taylor. In the west they made Dook'o'oosłííd, or San Francisco Peak. And in the north they fashioned Dibé Nitsaa, or Big Mountain Sheep. Those four mountains they built at the four cardinal points. Living there were holy people, a different kind of people, intelligent people who could ride the sunbeam and travel the rainbow and "nothing in any world could change the way they were."[8]

Once they had created the celestial and terrestrial environment of the Fifth World to their liking, the couple began to take on its many social and natural challenges. Now *Diné Bahane'* becomes a story about people: the gathering of the clans that would comprise the Navajo, the slaying of the monsters, and regaining of the supernaturals' trust. There is a pressing need to learn to live in *hózhó* (beauty, balance, and harmony)—but the path is fraught with tension and danger.

Will we ever learn to master our frailties? Are we truly meant to become socialized? Should we really attempt to become godlike? When does sexuality become destructive? Why should we marry? What is the nature of our kin in this world? These are some of the people-centered questions addressed in *Diné Bahane'*. As in *Theogony*, they are dealt with in a cyclic narrative, with an ebb and flow of action that is characterized by repeated encounter, dispersal, and renewal.

One very mischievous animal, sometimes helpful and at other times a troublemaker who sets things back, plays a central role in the story of how the Navajo people came to be civilized—Coyote. He plays the trickster, a kind of hero in Pan-American mythology. Coyote Trickster draws attention to opposing conflicting sides of human nature by forcing people to face situations they fear. For example, when people want to know what will become of them, he plays a game of heads or tails with them by throwing a stone into the water: "If it sinks, we will eventually perish. But if it floats, we shall all go on living," he tells them. When it sinks, everyone becomes angry. They threaten to throw Coyote in the river. "Wait!," he says:

> "Listen to me. If we all go on living, and if the women keep having babies, there will be too many people. There won't be any room. Nobody will be able to move around. There will be no place to plant corn. Isn't it better that each one of us should live here for just a while, until old age slows us down? Not just until we can't hunt. Not just until we can't plant and harvest. But until we can't think. Until we can no longer speak. Then we ought to move on. Leave everything behind for the young. Make room for the next generation."[9]

Sound wisdom from someone who grabs your attention by tossing a stone in the water. Grudgingly the people agree that Coyote is right. They all grow silent.

So what's the purpose of this so-called death segment in *Diné Bahane'*, which is just one of many so-called Coyote-cycle stories? This story, like others in the series, offers a lesson about false belief—situations we'd like to see versus things the way they really are. Coyote mocks real-life situations by displaying characteristics that we ought to avoid. He reveals the disharmony that young Earth-Surface People must learn to avoid as they organize into harmonious clans.

But why, of all animals, should the Coyote Trickster become such a central character in *Diné Bahane'*? To address that question, we need to think about how different cultures per-

Barrier Canyon–style rock drawings showing the animate forces of nature in Puebloan cosmology. (Thomas from USA / CC BY 2.0)

ceive the world they live in—in this case the behavior of real coyotes who abound in the U.S. Southwest.[10]

I think what makes it difficult for outsiders to warm to the Navajo version of creation is that the story blurs the distinction between animals and people. Even the word "people" is applied to creatures that are unlike humans today. The Air-Spirit People of the First World are described as being unlike the five-fingered Earth-Surface People who come into the world today. They travel in the air like our birds, visiting successive levels of worlds. When they reach the Swallow People of the Second World, who are domesticated enough to live in blue houses, the Air-Spirit People are asked why they came and answer, to see if there were "people" here like themselves, which seems confusing to modern listeners. Similarly, when they reach the Grasshopper People of the Third World and the closer-to-human-looking inhabitants of the Fourth World—those who cut their hair square in front and live in houses on the ground— the tribal bonding between visitor and native fails, though it comes progressively closer to being achieved. A tale of harmony that once was lacking will finally be achieved through the action of the participating characters. But all of the characters in *Diné Bahane'* are called *people.* There seems to be no clear-cut anatomical difference between animals and humans. That's because the Navajo word for "being" applies to all forms of life. Nor is there a clear distinction between nature and the supernatural. The clumsy earthly behavior of Coyote contrasts with his extraordinary ability to shift shapes.

A story that depicts humanity interwoven with other life forms conflicts with the Western dualistic way of thinking that imposes boundaries between human and animal, living and non-living. Consider the Judeo-Christian idea of man being created in God's image, and thereby being accorded mastery over earth's lesser inhabitants. In the Navajo way of thinking, humans have no such superior status. Instead they live in an animate universe filled with powerful spirits and they must work to mediate with animal-like deities to achieve order. In this world, the people-animal boundary is fully negotiable.[11]

4

Five Aztec Creations

L ike many other stories of beginnings, the Aztec tale of the Five Suns, which echoes and contrasts in interesting ways the Navajo Five Peoples stories, suggests that creation was not a simple task.[1] The gods, like the people who worship them, simply cannot get it right in their early attempts. As in the fairy tale of the ugly duckling, the hero Nanauatzin (The pimply one), who successfully pulls it off, is modest, unattractive, and unencumbered by finery. But he is brave and inwardly confident in his ability to accomplish the awesome task set before him—to make time begin by becoming the rising sun. With his own sacrifice, Nanauatzin embodies the Aztec emperor's quest for sacrificial blood to keep the sun in motion, which the emperor fulfills with his military—the Eagle Warriors who conquer rival cities in the warlike environment of Central Mexico just prior to European contact.

The Aztecs say that they too started out as a humble tribe of wanderers who came from the north, instructed by the gods to build their capital city, Tenochtitlan (today's Mexico City). That the action in their creation story should take place in nearby Teotihuacan seems appropriate. Teotihuacan, one of ancient America's great cities, boasted a population of more than 100,000 before it fell several centuries before the rise of the Aztecs, who emerged in the Lake Texcoco basin 50 kilometers (30 mi.) to the southwest. Teotihuacan was to the Aztecs as Mycenae was to the Greeks. As the early Aztec intruders wandered among its abandoned colossal pyramids surrounded by high mountains, they wondered, Might the great people who built these mountains have been our ancestors? So begins the story.

There had been many creations (suns). In the first, the Sun of Jaguar, the gods made a race of giants. They lived in caves, but when they proved incapable of tilling the land, the gods decided to destroy them and start the task anew. So they sent jaguars to eat the giants. Next, in the Sun of Wind, they created normal-sized people and placed them on the surface of the earth; but as time passed the people gradually became less civilized and frequently failed to honor their creators. The gods sent a fierce wind to blow them away, and transformed the survivors, who managed to cling to the trees, into monkeys. In the third creation attempt, the Sun of Fire-Rain, the people the gods created knew how to till the land, but they paid too little attention to it, especially when drought plagued their crops. Disgusted by the behavior of those they had worked so hard to create, the gods caused the volcanoes to erupt, sending down a rain of fire to do away with them. Those who escaped the flames were turned into birds. Then came the fourth sun—the Sun of Water. Unfortunately its people were too selfish, so they too needed to be done away with—this time by a flood from torrential downpours sent by the gods. The survivors were turned into fish. We live in the fifth sun, the Sun of Movement. The birth of the fifth sun happened at the ancient abandoned city of Teotihuacan, the place where time began. This was the home of the gods.

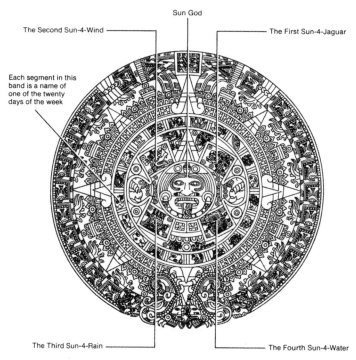

Sun God

The Second Sun-4-Wind

The First Sun-4-Jaguar

Each segment in this band is a name of one of the twenty days of the week

The Third Sun-4-Rain

The Fourth Sun-4-Water

The Aztec sun stone depicts the five creation epochs in cyclic time. The Sun of Movement is at the center. (A. Aveni, *Empires of Time: Calendars, Clocks, and Cultures* [New York: Basic, 1989])

When all was in darkness, when yet no sun had shown, the gods gathered there; they took counsel among themselves, and raised the question: Who will carry the burden? Who will take it upon himself to be the sun, to bring the dawn? The one named Tecuciztecatl (Tecciztecatl), the proud and pretentious Lord of the Snails, responded immediately: "I shall be the one!" Anyone else?, inquired the gods. No one stepped forward. To make it a competition, the gods decided to choose another among them. Surprisingly, they singled out a little-known, pimply-faced one, so-named Nanauatzin, who quietly stood listening at the side; he was among the humblest of all the gods. "Thou shalt be the one!," said the gods in unison. Nanauatzin immediately responded, "I heartily accept. You have always been good to me."

To begin the awesome task, Tecuciztecatl and Nanauatzin were each sent to one of the two Teotihuacan hills to fast and do penance for four days. Today you can still see these hills—we call them Pyramid of the Sun and Pyramid of the Moon. Meanwhile an immense fire was laid all the way around the rim of the Teotihuacan horizon. Tecuciztecatl came forth and offered for his penance fir branches made of quetzal bird feathers, grass balls of gold, maguey cactus spines of turquoise, and the finest aromatic incense. Poor Nanauatzin could give only fir branches made out of water rushes, green grass balls, and ordinary maguey spines. As for his incense, there were only the scabs of the sores with which he was afflicted.

At midnight ending the fourth day, the sacrificants were given their adornments: for Tecuciztecatl a forked heron headdress and sleeveless jacket, and for Nanauatzin a headdress, stole, and loincloth—all fashioned out of plain paper. Next the gods arranged themselves in a double line at the center of Teotihuacan. They set Tecuciztecatl and Nanauatzin in the center, facing the blazing hearth surrounding them. Then they spoke in unison to Tecuciztecatl: "Take courage, Tecuciztecatl—cast thyself into the fire!" So charged, he ran forward to hurl himself into the flames. Soon the intense heat began to reach him; it was insufferable, intolerable, unbearable. It practically melted his skin. The closer he drew, the higher the flames flared. Tecuciztecatl became terrified; he halted in fear, turned around, and retreated. He screwed up enough courage to give it another try. But a second time he was compelled to leap back. A third try and a fourth—all failed. Tecuciztecatl was defeated. He slunk away in disgrace.

Now it was Nanauatzin's turn to respond to the call: "Onward, thou O Nanauatzin! Take heart." And Nanauatzin, determined and resolved, hardened his heart, and firmly shut his eyes. He had no fear; he did not stop short; he did not falter in fright; he did not turn back. He quickly cast himself into the fire, whereupon he burned; his body crackled and sizzled. When Tecuciztecatl saw what happened, he too cast himself into the fire and burned. But too little too late, for only the first to enter the flames could become the sun. From this sacrifice the Aztec people take the custom where one who is valiant is called a *quauhtlocelotl*, a warrior, for they also saw an eagle (*quauhtl*) and an ocelot (*ocelotl*) follow Nanauatzin into the fire.

Now all the gods sat in darkness waiting to see where Nanauatzin would rise and become the sun. There they all sat, waiting for the dawn. They waited a long time. Then there began the reddening of the dawn in all directions. The gods fell upon their knees to await where he who had become the sun would come to rise. In all directions they looked; everywhere they peered and kept turning about. Some thought that it would be from the north, so they looked that way; some did the same to the west; some to the south; and some to the east. They were seeing light everywhere, so maybe he would rise in all directions? But true were the words of those who looked east—Quetzalcoatl (Learning), Ehecatl (Wind), and the others who were destined to become the gods of the Aztec ancestors, there at Teotihuacan—saying, "There in that place, the sun will come to rise."

When the sun finally burst forth, he appeared red; he kept swaying unsteadily from side to side. It was impossible to look into his face; he blinded one with his light, so intensely did he shine. He issued rays of light from himself in all directions; his brilliant rays penetrated everywhere. The gods steadied him, and moderated his brightness. Then Tecuciztecatl came to rise, following behind the newly created sun in the east. They say that originally the two were equally dazzling, but when the gods saw that, they said: "How may this be? Will they both together follow the same path? Will they both shine like this?" Realizing that this surely could not happen, one of the gods grabbed hold of a rabbit and flung it at the face of Tecuciztecatl's second sun, darkening its face, killing its brilliance. So he became the full moon. Look closely and you can still see the dark markings of the rabbit on its face.

But still, neither the sun nor the moon could move. The two stood motionless, one above the other at the east horizon. Then Ehecatl, God of Wind, came forward. He exerted himself fiercely and violently as he blew. Slowly the sun began to move and go on his way. Ehecatl blew fiercely a second time and by the time the sun had reached the opposite horizon, the moon too began to move, but at a different rate. So the two passed each other and went on their way. Thus the sun comes forth once and spends the whole day in his work; and the full moon undertakes the night's task. From this it seems that the moon, Tecuciztecatl, could have been the sun if he had been first to cast himself into the fire. After all, he had presented himself first and all his offerings had been costly in the penances. But alas, he failed to act at his most crucial moment.

And when thus their work was done, the gods said: "Let it be that through us the sun may always be revived. Now let all of us die." So today we offer sacrifice to the gods in debt payment for creating the Sun of Movement. It all happened there in Teotihuacan. Here ends the legend, which was told in times past, and has ever since resided in the keeping of the old people.

The lesson involving the death of the gods is about reciprocity. Just as exchanges of gifts establish hierarchical relationships between chiefs and vassals in the military state, sacrifice sets up the same between gods and worshippers. The Aztecs believed that the universe belonged to the gods who sacrificed to create space-time for them. Thus they facilitate the eternal exchange that prevents the disruption of cycles of time: wet/dry, life/ death, and appearance/disappearance of things in the sky, such as the sun and the moon. The greater the gift, the more stable the world is destined to become. Under the domain of the Aztec imperial state of the late fourteenth to early fifteenth centuries, blood sacrifice, especially to their patron god of sun and war, Huitzilopochtli, was paramount. Only through the blood of sacrifice from captives acquired in warfare could the continuation of the fifth sun of creation be sustained. These sacrifices were conducted in the Aztec Templo Mayor, the most prominent among the temples of Tenochtitlan. If the habit of offering blood stopped, the fifth, and final, sun would be destroyed—this time through gigantic earthquakes, as its name, Sun of Movement, suggests. The environment of Mexico City, plagued by frequent earthquakes and surrounded by mountains, including the smoking volcano Popocatépetl (the likely inspiration for an earlier destruction by a rain of fire), was the perfect backdrop for the action of this unique creation story.

5

Creation Battles in the Andean Highlands

I n the Andes of South America, all things are recognized by their place in an up-and-down environment. To understand why, take a car or bus trip from the Pacific coast of Peru to the highlands. You'll experience extraordinary variations in Andean ecology in a single day, as you rise within a few hours from the lush lowland region to the frigid highland plains where llama herders dwell. The ethos of balance and order that Andean anthropologists call the "complementary dualism of verticality" is peculiar to such mountain-based cultures.[1] Take the competition between lowland agriculturists and highland herders. The Inca empire, which was in full flower between the late fifteenth and early sixteenth centuries, stretched along three parallel mountain chains from Ecuador to Chile, and was highly organized according to this up-versus-down paradigm. Its creation story celebrates the victory of the civilized highland mountain-storm-water fertility deity Paria Caca—bringer of civilization—over Huallallo Caruincho, the lowland cannibalistic god of fire. The tale is told by the Yauyos, people of the Peruvian highlands, who regard themselves as the proud descendants of the Inca, who defeated and subjugated the Yunca, or lowland, coastal people prior to the sixteenth-century European invasion. The steep environment from highland to coast where these people lived sets the stage for the principal tension between highlander and lowlander— who will control the water?[2]

The major actors in the battle are *huacas.* A huaca is any material thing endowed with superhuman characteristics. It can be a mountain, a spring, a rock outcrop, a ruined building, a tree, an animal—even a mummified ancestor. Unlike our contemporary world, the world of the Yauyos makes no distinction between matter and spirit. And Yauyos heroes, unlike many other supernatural beings, act within rather than outside nature. It is easy to see that the major actors in this grassroots mythology derive from the Andean landscape.

Long ago there were only superpowered sacred beings we call huacas that made up the landscape. Two huacas from the coast, Yana Ñamca and Tuta Ñamca, made the first people; but they were defeated by the fire monster Huallallo Caruincho, also called the Man Eater, the Man Drinker. It was he who ordered the first people to bear two children and no more. He would eat one of them, while the parents could raise whichever one they loved better. In those times people came back to life five days after they died, and their crops ripened exactly five days after they were planted. The aboriginal people called themselves the Yunca. Eventually a great number of them began to populate the warm valleys along the coast. To scratch out a living, they started digging into the rock faces of the adjacent mountains. You can still see the remains of their terraced fields today.

Unfortunately the world wanted to come to an end. The sun went dark for five days and the rocks in the highlands began

Paria Caca, Andean mountain god of water and storms, wearing
his majestic cloak of snow. (Cordillera Pariacaca CC BY 3.0)

to bang together. The ocean wanted to overflow and inundate
the land. You'd better go to the highlands, to the mountain
Villca Coto, if you want to be saved, warned the huacas. Sadly
only a few of the Yunca made it to the peak, which was already
crowded with foxes, llamas, and condors—all kinds of animals
in great numbers. The ensuing flood exterminated nearly all
the people. When the land finally dried out, the people started
to multiply once more. Those who survived on Villca Coto
Mountain became our ancestors.

　　These uncivilized people spent a lot of time at war with
one another. They recognized only the strong and the wealthy
as their leaders. It was at this time that the huaca called Paria
Caca, god of water and rainstorms, was born out of the eggs
of five falcons in the highlands on the mountain Condor Coto.
He would later become human, travel the world, and seek to

civilize the people. But first he would need to engage in a colossal battle with Huallallo Caruincho. For this task he sent his
son, Huatya Curi.

Huatya Curi was very modest. He was also poor; he
dressed in rags and, because he needed to eat the way poor
people do, the Yauyos, or highland people, called him the
Baked Potato Gleaner.[3] But Huatya Curi also knew the ways
of all the animals and he was very clever. He showed it when,
in his travels, he encountered a rich man named Tamta Ñamca,
who had spent his life deceiving lots of people by making them
believe he was their god. Unfortunately, Tamta Ñamca's health
was no match for his wealth. He had contracted and lived with
a horrible mysterious disease for many years. People wondered
how could a man who is so rich, who knows so much, who's so
powerful, be so sick? Despite summoning many doctors and
shamans, no diagnosis could be found.

When Huatya Curi happened to pass through the foothills, he came across a group of foxes. When he asked them
what was going on, they told him: there's a sick man in that
town who's been pretending to be a god. As Huatya Curi approached the opulent residence of Tamta Ñamca, he encountered a young woman and asked her: "Is someone sick in this
town?" She replied, "It's my father who's sick." "I'll cure your father," Huatya Curi responded. They then went inside the house
and the girl said, "Father, there's a poor man here. He came
and said to me, 'I'll cure your father.'" Hearing this, all the wise
men sitting around the lord's bedside burst into laughter. "If
we ourselves can't cure him, how can this nobody make him
well?" But Tamta Ñamca was in such pain that he responded,
"Let him come, never mind what sort of man he is."[4]

When the wealthy lord summoned him to his bedside,
Huatya Curi told him that he would make him well only if he
promised him his daughter's hand. Tamta Ñamca was over-

joyed at the offer, but when Anchi Cocha, the rich husband of the lord's older daughter, heard the proposition, he flew into a rage: "How dare a nobody like you marry the sister-in-law of such a powerful man as me?" Then he muttered under his breath, "I'll bring deep shame on that beggarman!" So the brother-in-law challenged Huatya Curi. "Let's have a drinking and dancing contest!," he said.[5] The rich man went first. He danced an impressive dance with two hundred women to the music of his own pan-pipe orchestra. When he finished, the poor man performed, accompanied by his soon-to-be wife and a skunk who played the drum—but a very special drum, for once the beat was under way, the mountains all around them quaked. With this impressive dance he beat them all.

Next came a maize-beer drinking contest. As a guest, Huatya Curi sat at the head of the group and all the others seated around served drink after drink of the host's beer without a break. Even though they all drank every bit of what was served, there were no problems. Then it was Huatya Curi's turn. He began to serve guests the maize beer he brought in a tiny long-necked jar. "How could he possibly fill so many people from such a tiny jar?," they ridiculed him.[6] But this was a very special bottomless jar. As he poured and poured, they drank and drank. One by one they all dropped down and soon no one was left upright except Huatya Curi. He had won again! Deceived by trickery, the angry brother-in-law insisted on another contest—this time a dress-up competition. The rich man put on his finest puma skins and impressed all the onlookers. Then Huatya Curi donned his father's snow garment, which dazzled everyone, especially when the outer layers of it changed to water, which flew off into the sky and made the final rainbow— just like the ones we see today.

Exasperated, the rich brother-in-law insisted on one more contest—house building. Since the rich man had access to many helpers, he nearly finished the entire house in a day. Meanwhile poor Huatya Curi, working only with his companion, barely managed to lay the foundation by sunset. But when the next day dawned, the challenger was awestruck when he beheld Huatya Curi's fully finished beautiful house, for in the night all kinds of birds, snakes, and other animals had walled off the residence. The guanacos and vicuñas (llama-like camelids) had brought his thatching straight down from the mountains. A bobcat helped: he chased the guanacos and vicuñas and in the stampede, the shaking and quaking of their hooves caused the rich man's house to fall down. "Go, idiot," said Huatya Curi to his wealthy adversary. "You have victimized me so much, I'll kill you!"[7] And he chased the brother-in-law and his wife all the way down the mountains to the coast. There the man turned into a brocket deer and disappeared; but Huatya Curi caught Anchi Cocha's wife on the road, stood her upside down, and turned her to stone.[8] She's the mountain pass you come through today on your way up to the highlands.

Then Huatya Curi returned to the town and completed his promise to cure Tamta Ñamca. It turns out he was afflicted by a pair of snakes who lived on top of his dwelling and a two-headed toad who resided under his grinding stone: "Now we'll kill them. Then you'll get well. . . . And as for you, you're not such a powerful man? That's just not true!"[9] So the rich man— now humbled but grateful for the cure—offered Huatya Curi his unmarried daughter. Thus Huatya Curi, having learned how to defeat his enemies through trickery, was ready for his most demanding task—the inevitable battle with the Fire Monster and Man Eater, Huallallo Caruincho.

Early on the morning of the day of battle, Huallallo Caruincho blazed up out of his volcano in the form of a giant fire that reached almost all the way up to the heavens. Huatya Curi began to wage the battle by raining down from five directions, one for each of his persons—just like his father, for he too had been born of five eggs. It was a yellow and red rain. Flashing lightning also blazed down from five directions. But Huallallo Caruincho would not let himself be extinguished. Meanwhile the rains of Huatya Curi rushed down toward the ocean. There was so much water it couldn't fit, and the level of the ocean began to rise and inundate the land. Then one of Huatya Curi's five selves knocked down a mountain and dammed the waters from below. He made an immense lake and, as the waters filled it, they surrounded and nearly quenched the fires of Huallallo Caruincho. Relentlessly Huatya Curi kept flashing lightning bolts at his foe, not allowing him a moment to rest.

Finally exhausted and burned out, Huallallo Caruincho fled to the low country, never to be seen in highland Yauyos territory again. Huatya Curi banished all his Yunca worshippers with him as well. Then, right there in the highlands, Huatya Curi established his cult, made up of lineages that descended from his fivefold self. He established his dwelling on the top of the mountain that carries his name. There he set up his rules of worship, telling his people they were all of one birth—one family. And he instructed the chiefs of each highland village to organize a celebration once a year to reenact his life. It would happen at the time when the sun's rays touch a certain calibrated wall, casting no shadow. They say that many years later, when the Christians came to the highlands, they fixed this celebration so that it coincided with their major Eastertime feast.[10]

6

Salt of the Earth

AMAZONIAN BEGINNINGS

Diasporic or migrating people—those who change place—have to connect the story of where they came from with the tale of where they end up. Anthropologists call this process "placemaking," and it often makes the relation between culture and landscape complicated. For the Southern Arawak people of western Amazonia, the landscape is said to have originated out of divine action, before the world became differentiated into the features that we see today. The forces that created the landscape have remained alive and continue to reshape the earth as they interact with people and animals.

Long sacred to the Southern Arawak people is a place called Cerro de la Sal (Salt hill), located at the junction of the Posapno and Entaz rivers. It was created out of the transformed body of Pareni, the salt goddess, the one who gave people a substance of many types to add to their foods in order to nourish them and to make what they eat taste better, like *yapa pos* (agouti salt) or *ma'yarro pos* (jaguar salt). Most valuable of these edible salts was *queñtot pos,* or red salt. There were also inedible salts to watch out for, like *toma pos* (parrot salt) and *errasañatsa pos* (blood salt).

The Yanesha live where the jungle of the Amazon basin meets the Andean foothills in central Peru. Their creation story explains the origin of the salt of the earth, and gives us a mental mineral map of their sacred space. It was because of the transformative actions of the gods in what was once un-bounded space that the Yanesha ultimately found the place where they reside today. The characters in their creation story trace the migratory route that brought them there.[1]

They say that in the beginning, humans, animals, spirits, and gods—all were immortal. They lived in humanlike form and shared the earth together, though not always harmoniously. At that time the evil deity Yompor Rret ruled the heavens. He lit up the sky of the primeval earth and took special pleasure in killing people. Out of compassion, the benevolent god Yom-por Ror set out to dethrone Yompor Rret, then ascend into the sky to replace him as the new sun. But Yompor Ror's older sib-lings, who came along to help out, became excited as the plan unfolded, and carelessly ran ahead of him. This angered Yom-por Ror and caused him to lose control of himself. He prema-turely triggered his powers of transformation en route to the mountain Cheporepen, the point from where he had planned his ascent into the sky.

First Yompor Ror transformed the primordial forms of animals and plants into those the Yanesha know today. The streams in the valley of Cheporepen where he encountered them still bear their names. Yompor Ror then transformed into stone some primordial Yanesha he met along the way who had failed to display the moral virtues he believed in—a man who refused to share the fish he had caught and smoked downriver, and a group of travelers who declined to share the beautifully colored parrots they had captured. You can see their figures too if you look closely at the sharp white cliffs where the mountains descend to the jungle and in the crouching boulders that have rolled down along the banks of the Chorobamba River. Had Yompor Ror not arrived so late on the scene, maybe this area wouldn't be so poor for fishing today.

When Yompor Ror caught up to his older siblings, he turned them to stone as well. One of them, a small white polished stone, was later stolen by the white people. A mighty struggle with another of them caused the vegetation on the surrounding hills to be denuded by a huge fire. Still today they are covered only with tall grass. This is how the earth received its present shape. When Yompor Ror finally reached the mountain Cheporepen, he ascended into heaven and was followed by the other divinities. Thus ended the time of sociability between humans and the gods, who became the stars and constellations.

Later in pre-social times the earth was a powerful deity, a female called Kipátsi. She could create all the things that exist in the world out of her divine breath. Among the deities who had the greatest influence on her was Pareni, the original human form of salt, who was born with extraordinary powers of transformation. Pareni married several times but, unfortunately, she always seemed to have bad luck. She was repeatedly forced to transform her husbands into present-day animals— one became a hummingbird, another a dung beetle, a third a sweat bee . . . until she married the primordial armadillo, Kinteroni. He possessed transformative powers nearly equal to her own. He and his evil brother, Pachakamui, went around transforming into animals practically every being they encountered in the first world—monkeys, deer, and tapirs. They even transformed Pareni's sons into fish. Indeed, the brothers became so intoxicated with their extraordinary powers that they ended up accidentally transforming themselves—Kinteroni into a giant armadillo, Pachakamui into a palm tree. Streams where all of these changes took place still bear their names.

Now Pareni was desolate. All of her children, with the exception of one daughter, had been changed into animals. With her daughter she undertook a long journey to seek out a place where she could peacefully raise her fish-children. Down the Urubamba and up the Tambo and Perene rivers she went, passing through lands occupied by other tribes. They say that wherever she stopped along the way to urinate, salty springs originated; so did salt deposits and clays containing an abundance of salt. The places still bear the names: there's Chimiato (Water of the salt pit), Tivíha (Salt spring), and Potiaríni (Salty water). Finally, Pareni and her daughter settled in the Upper Perene. There, in her last act, she transformed herself and her daughter into salt mines. Today the people can remember where they came from by following Pareni's journey. And you can visit the goddess today—she is a large hill called Pareni in Matsiguenga territory. It's marked by a wide vein of reddish salt. At the bottom of this hill runs the salty water of the Tiviari (Salt river). Standing next to her mother is Pareni's daughter: a smaller hill that contains a vein of white salt. The whole story is written in the landscape.

PART TWO

WATERWAYS

Before creation there was only chaos, a kind of emptiness or void—a gap, a chasm, an abyss. It was there before the earth and the sky, once united, became separated. No one had ever experienced such a formlessness. To judge by the words used in many myths to describe beginnings, modern cosmologists still think of the inception of the universe that way—a primordial, incomprehensible state of confusion at the very instant the Big Bang happened fourteen billion years ago. We can acquire no true knowledge of such a state of affairs. We can only imagine chaos as an insensible, unmeasurable state of high temperature and high density all confined to a point—a singularity. Whatever it had been, it was quickly separated into matter and energy, the way the primordial waters or primordial darkness—equivalent terms for chaos in other creation stories—could replace disorder with order. One significant difference is that in the modern version of the creation myth, there is no describable agency behind what took place—no "first cause." But as we shall see when we encounter the struggle for order in the midst of chaos in *Enuma Elish*, the oldest known creation story from the Middle East, the great separation emerges in personified form out of a battle between a heroic deity, the sweet water that flows in the Tigris-Euphrates, and a monster of chaos, the salt water of the Persian Gulf. The battle occurs where the two waters meet.

Like the Babylonian *Enuma Elish,* the Egyptian creation myth is based on the flow of water. All things originate along the banks of the stream of life—the Nile River. There the parents of the world are born out of a cosmic egg deposited in the *benben,* one of many mounds of silt visible along the banks of the Nile River delta at the end of the seasonal flood. Just as the mountains surrounding Teotihuacan would become the great pyramids of Mexico, the benben form would evolve into the great pyramids of Egypt, eternal monuments built by the people to house their deceased pharaoh, living descendant of the sun god on earth.

On the other side of Africa, the tribal Mande people also tell a story of creation from an egg, except that the shell—the placenta from which combative twin deities emerge like seeds from a pod—plays as seminal a role as its contents. The body of the victorious twin is transformed into the odd boomerang-like course of the Niger River, which dramatically shifts its direction of flow in the midst of a desert and becomes the Inner Delta, a land of shallow marshes teeming with fish.

Traveling along a coastline is a bit like navigating a river with a single bank. The creation hero of the Tlingit tribal elders of the northwest U.S. and Canadian coast is the Raven, who behaves a lot like the Navajo Coyote—a traveler-transformer. He paddles his canoe close to shore, effortlessly changing from bird to plant to person and back as he comes in contact with coastal inhabitants and performs fantastic feats to make manifest their basic needs: light, fresh water, shellfish, and salmon.

7

Enuma Elish

CONTROLLING THE WATERS

What is the closest condition you can experience that evokes the formless, indescribably confused state we call chaos—the condition that supposedly existed before order came into the world? A hurricane or tornado? Maybe a blizzard or an erupting volcano? Is it the bottom of a dark and turbulent ocean, perhaps a torrential river in the midst of a flood? I think it depends on your own sphere of experience. If you live in the arid region around where the Tigris and Euphrates empty into the Persian Gulf, chaos could well be imagined as a violent sandstorm.

The *shamal* (Arabic for north) is a northwesterly wind that blows over today's Iraq, especially during seasons when the polar jet stream slips southward and encroaches on its subtropical counterpart. Together the two generate winds up to 80 kilometers per hour (50 mph) that precede dry cold fronts. The major shamal happens about two months after the spring equinox, its arrival heralded by the constellation Thorayya (the Pleiades) setting in the west just before dawn. People still call this shamal Al Haffar Sarih Thorayya (Pleiades driller), after the huge *haffar* (depressions) it drills in the sand dunes. Shamals have been known to go on for several days, closing roads and businesses and overwhelming hospital emergency rooms with people suffering respiratory ailments. When the blinding, blowing sand encounters the turbulent waters of the Gulf in the Euphrates delta, the chaos is transformed into an impenetrable mist of sand and fog. Fishermen stay in port; they say that this storm devours ships.

A month later the last shamal of spring, Al Dabaran (the follower), arrives, again timed by the stars—the last appearance of the bright star Aldebaran, which slips out of view about one month after the Pleiades. This storm lasts several days and keeps people hiding indoors, often with the windows taped shut to escape the extremely fine dust brought down from the mountains of Syria and Turkey. (Winter shamals also take place, twice or three times a month, but they are less persistent.)

Now try to imagine the intermingling fresh and salt waters amid the hazy shamal. This is precisely the environment depicted in the opening lines of the creation myth recounted here—a story most often told at the beginning of spring, the new year. Like the Judeo-Christian Passover/Easter, this is a time to celebrate the restoration of life following the winter deluge and to warn of any adversity that might impinge on the new cycle of life.

When Babylon came to power in the Tigris-Euphrates valley under King Hammurabi (r. 1792–1750 BCE), Marduk, God of War and Storms, had become the city's national deity. At the end of the spring Akitu festival, citizens assembled at the Esagila, the temple dedicated to him.[1] They stood before a statue of Marduk, where the story of creation, written on seven giant clay tablets (now lost) erected beside the effigy, was recited by the high priest. It is called *Enuma Elish,* or "When on high," after the opening words of an oral hand-me-down story that was later inscribed in cuneiform.[2] The opening scene describes the chaotic environment in which the world was created.

There were no pastures then, "not (even) a reed marsh [is] to be seen," where Apsu (male—sweet water) and Tiamat (female—salt water) come together.[3] Out of their union the couple create five generations of descendants, among them Enlil, god of the air, and Ea, who represents time—which cannot begin to flow until earth and sky are separated. Family tensions arise: Ea is threatened by his father but does away with him by performing an overpowering holy incantation that puts Apsu to sleep—but not before Tiamat asks that rhetorical question many pose to their creator: "Why should we destroy that which we ourselves have brought forth?"[4]

The line of descent ultimately passes to Marduk, the youngest son. Like Zeus in the *Theogony,* he must overcome his ultimate enemy, who turns out to be his avenging mother. Only then can Marduk be permitted to ascend to the position of chief god of the city of Babylon. The battle is reminiscent of the encounter between Zeus and Typhoeus in the Greek *Theogony,* which likely derived in part from the older Babylonian myth as it migrated across the Aegean. It ends with the slaying of Tiamat—often reenacted in Babylon before a live audience:

When Tiamat opened her mouth to devour him
He drove in the evil wind, in order that (she should)
not (be able) to close her lips.

The raging winds filled her belly;
Her belly became distended and she opened wide her
mouth.

Marduk slays Tiamat in the battle between fresh water and salt
water. (Austen Henry Layard, "Bas-reliefs at an entrance to a small
temple [Nimroud]," *A Second Series of the Monuments of Nineveh,*
General Research Division, The New York Public Library Digital
Collections, http://digitalcollections.nypl.org/items/510d47dc
-4726-a3d9-e040-e00a18064a99, accessed May 4, 2020)

> He shot off an arrow, and it tore her interior.
> It cut through her inward parts, it split (her) heart . . .
> When he had subdued her, he destroyed her life.[5]

Out of her carcass Marduk creates the heavens, being
careful to control the water that might unexpectedly descend
from above:

> He split her open like a mussel (?) into two (parts);
> Half of her he set in place and formed the sky
>   (therewith)
> as a roof.

> He fixed the crossbar (and) posted guards;
> He commanded them not to let her waters escape.[6]

Once Marduk sets up the stations for the gods, he creates the rest of the universe—again with due attention to controlling the water:

> The stars their likeness(es), the signs of the zodiac, he
>   set up.
> He determined the year, defined the divisions;
> For each of the twelve months he set up three
>   constellations.
> After he had def[ined] the days of the year [by means]
>   of constellations,
> He founded the station of Nîbiru [the equinox] to make
>   known their duties(?).
> That none might go wrong (and) be remiss,
> He established the stations of Enlil and Ea together
>   with it.
> He opened gates on both sides,
> And made strong lock(s) to the left and to the right.
> In the very center thereof he fixed the zenith.
> The moon he caused to shine forth; the night he en-
>   trusted (to her).
> He appointed her, the ornament of the night, to make
>   known the days.
> "Monthly without ceasing go forth, with a tiara" [the
>   crescent phase, which begins the month of lunar
>   phases].[7]

Finally, Marduk gets around to creating people. He delegates this less important task to his associates, who fashion them out of clay bound by the blood of the defeated enemy. To what end? Clearly, this universe was created for the gods, not us. As you might imagine had you been living in an authoritarian theocracy, the gods need to be freed up to do more important things "not suited to human understanding." Workers needed! So "he imposed the services of the gods (upon them) and set the gods free."[8]

And the job description? Man shall assist in creating the Esagila Temple, to fashion its brickwork, to wield the hoe, to establish and maintain the sanctuary and its many shrines to make offerings at the appropriate times, and to learn to be in awe of the gods. *Enuma Elish* gives us a good idea of the civic environment in which the patriotic, if threatened, citizen of Babylon resided.

The lesson behind the fantastic imagery in *Enuma Elish*, with gods interacting like people, is that divine kingship lies at the root of the successful state. And this kingship must be established authoritatively—once and for all—through compulsive force. Likewise, a process of violent struggle is necessary to create an orderly universe. Apsu and Tiamat are what is old— they represent inertia, stasis, and inaction—while the deities of the younger generation introduce change and movement into the picture. They become the active agents of transformation of the world.

In *Enuma Elish*, creation is conceived as an act of separation. Things don't simply materialize out of nothing; some essence or potential—chaos—is already present. Originally the sky and the earth were one, formed out of the union of Apsu and Tiamat—with silt slowly and gradually being deposited and built up in the delta, accumulating all the way to the horizon as it accompanies the sweet river water down to the salty sea. By contrast, the force of the winds blowing down the Tigris-Euphrates valleys keeps earth and sky apart in a universe completely surrounded by water—ground water, water from the sky, and water from the rivers and the sea. It's a dynamic place of creation that is very different from the placid watery environment described earlier in the story.

What a sensible, poetic way for the Babylonians, inventors of trigonometry and the 360-degree circle, to think about the passage of time in their agrarian landscape—flowing steadily and slowly as the rich silt of the delta creates a nurturing land in the place where the waters mix. The heavy winter rains create a watery chaos: they cause the rivers to overflow their banks. But in the spring, when strong winds blow the clouds away, the waters of earth and heaven are parted and the sun, Marduk's celestial parallel and his source of power, dries out the land, restores order, creates life. Planting in the rich soil by the rivers can now commence. But beware the shamal, that omnipresent threat to the order of nature. Here then are two different stories of creation interwoven in the same myth—one placid, the other violent. Each represents both society and the natural landscape. Both scenarios are experienced in every season of the year. And both are true. Myth is reality.

8

The Nile from
Benben to Pyramid

When summer monsoons bring torrential rain to the Ethiopian highlands 3,000 kilometers (1,900 mi.) southeast of Egypt, most of the water flows into the Nile, carrying with it tons of sediment. The ancient Egyptians learned to anticipate the *akhet,* the annual inundation of the Nile. The hieroglyph for akhet, which also means "the place where the sun rises," shows a sun disk in a depression between two peaks.[1] The Egyptians could time the flood like clockwork because it happened every year just after Sothis, the bright star Sirius, reappeared in the east before sunrise, which in 3000 BCE occurred in early June. That was when readings on gauges set up on so-called nilometers installed upriver at the first cataract in Aswan, 600 kilometers (375 mi.) south of the Great Pyramids, began to rise. The Nile would swell dramatically—up to 8 meters (25 ft.) in depth through the summer—inundating the papyrus reeds and other vegetation along its banks. In September, when the flood began to recede, it would leave behind masses of fertile alluvial silt in the form of mounds of new land, called *benben.*

The Nile at night. The great waterway is a lifeline to all
those living within the vast Sahara desert. (NASA)

Living along the Nile, bordered by vast expanses of dry
desert on either bank, inspired the early Egyptians to think of it
as the stream of life and of the benben that seemed magically to
arise from its primeval waters as the source of creation. From
the benben emerged the earth god, who gave form to all that
we eat and offer the gods—good things. Indeed, the primeval
mound shape would inspire the gigantic pyramids that came
to dominate the built landscape. Because the benben was the
experienced source of the cycle of life and death, its imitation
in the form of a pyramid became the logical place to house the
mortal remains of a deceased monarch—a living descendent
of the sun god. Accompanied by his earthly needs—furniture
included—the pharaoh would be launched from the pyramid into the afterworld following the course of the dying sun,
which had originally emerged out of the benben. But where
exactly did the primeval mound that gave rise to all living

things first appear in the landscape? That depends on who tells the story.

The priests of Heliopolis say the benben was first seen precisely where their city borders the Nile.[2] That was where the god Atum, Lord of Heliopolis and "finisher of the world," the "one who came to be of himself," first emerged. Out of his own bodily fluids Atum immediately produced the God of Wisdom (Thoth) along with the gods of Air (Shu) and Moisture (Tefnut):

> When I had come into being, being (itself) came into being, and all beings came into being after I came into being. Many were the beings which came forward. . . . I was the one who copulated with my fist, I masturbated with my hand. Then I spewed with my own mouth. I spat out what was Shu, and I sputtered out what was Tefnut.[3]

Then Shu (dry air) and Tefnut (moist air) together produced Geb (Earth) and Nut (Sky), who would become the parents of the world. Now, Geb and Nut were so closely intertwined that Atum worried about the possibility of an illicit relation between them. Feeling the urgent need to separate them, he ordered Shu to stand firmly on Geb and thrust Nut above his head. But Nut had already become pregnant, which angered Atum all the more. He thus decreed that Nut would be forbidden to deliver her child on any of the 360 days of the year. Out of sympathy Thoth sought to help Nut. Gambling for more time, he challenged the other gods to a checker tournament. He won five days, which he added to the year, making it 365 days long. That gave Nut enough time to give birth to five children: the gods of Order (Osiris) and Disorder (Seth), as well as the Mother Goddess (Isis), her sister, Protector of the Dead (Nephthys), and a son, Horus, who would become guardian of the pharaoh—ultimately the pharaoh himself. All together, beginning with Atum, the nine Egyptian deities would come to be known as the Ennead (Group of Nine) of Heliopolis.

Another storyteller—this one from Hermopolis—offers a different version of events. Before the sacred benben was even formed, four pairs of male and female deities, known as the Ogdoad, or Group of Eight, already dwelled in the primeval waters. The males were frogs and the females snakes (or baboons). Nun and Naunet were the primeval ocean without form; Heh and Hauhet were manifestations of infinity; Kek and Kauket represented darkness; and Amun and Amaunet were the incarnations of two forms of hidden power—everything in pairs. The Group of Eight all remained hidden, for they were the antithesis of life, though because they were paired sexually, they also held the power of the possibility of life.[4]

Suddenly an unexplained cataclysm occurred. In an instant the two sexes were driven together.[5] The violent clash created the original primordial mound—the benben at the water's edge. Within it lodged a cosmic egg. It slowly began to crack open and out of it emerged Ra, the youthful sun god. As soon as he exited, remnants of his shell instantly burst into flames. With that, the newly born sun god flew up into the sky. This was the very first sunrise to take place in the world and it happened at Hermopolis, where the Ogdoad became the father-mothers who created the Egyptian sun god.

But Ra was not destined to experience a carefree life. He would be forever immersed in a struggle to keep his rightful place in heaven. Every dusk, when he reached the Land of the Dead on the western horizon, he was stalked by the indestructible Apophis, God of Darkness, the embodiment of the evil forces that dwelt beneath the ocean that surrounded the world.

There Apophis waited, coiled up like a serpent, for Ra's sky barque to enter his turf. Apophis's nightly aim was to keep Ra from passing through the underworld on his way to rise in the east to start the next day. If Apophis succeeded in the nightly battle, the balance of forces between good and evil would be overturned. The world would return to a state of primeval water, with a flood destroying the world, leaving things as they were before creation. But if Ra appeared, victorious in the east, security from the cosmic threat would be guaranteed—at least for another day.

Ra needed all the help he could get from both his heavenly family and his incarnate form as pharaoh in order to repel the chaotic force of the dragon of the night. This magical spell survives from a papyrus text:

> This spell is to be recited over Apophis drawn on a new sheet of papyrus in green color and put inside a box on which his name is set, he being tied and bound and put on the fire every day, wiped out with thy left foot and spat upon four times in the course of every day. Thou shalt say as thou puttest him on the fire: "Re (Ra) is triumphant over thee, O Apophis!"—four times . . . and "Pharaoh—life, prosperity, health!—is triumphant over his enemies."[6]

Water and the sun lie at the center of all variations of the Egyptian story of creation. But creation was not a one-time affair. It was an eternal, ongoing, cyclic process, as every Egyptian who ever experienced the daily sunrise and the annual flood knew.

Dynastic Egyptian creation stories are all about the godly origins of royalty. Much like in *Theogony* and *Enuma Elish*, we hear next to nothing about where ordinary people came from.

But one story from the upper reaches of the Nile, the part that connects with the alluvial deposits that create the benben, tells of Khnum, god of craftsmanship, who used a potter's wheel to make people out of clay formed from the silt and mud of the Nile. He built skulls and molded cheeks to give the face its shape, then added a spine to keep his creation upright, lungs to breathe with, guts for digestion, and genitalia to reproduce.

The theme of the benben as a source of creation is well traveled along the Nile. The contemporary Shilluk tribe of South Sudan, who live on the Nile's west bank, tell of their creator god, Juok, who collected different kinds of mud and soil all along the Nile to create the various races of the world.[7] In the north he used the abundant white sand and silt to mold white people. Farther south, up the Nile, he used darker soils to create red and brown people. In the land of the Shilluks, he made black people out of the rich, dark earth found on its banks. He equipped all of his creations with arms, legs, ears, eyes, and other body parts so that they could prosper. The power of the Nile is universal.

9

The Mande and the
River Niger

The Niger is the longest river in West Africa. Its odd boomerang-shaped course begins within 250 kilometers (155 mi.) of the Atlantic Ocean in the silt-free mountains of Sierra Leone, then turns inland to the northeast and breaks up into a series of marshes and streams, where it loses water to evaporation. This is where it enters the southern Sahara Desert, in southwestern Mali. There the so-called Inner Niger Delta, which contains the 320 kilometer (200 mi.)–long Lake Débo, interrupts the regular flow. The river's course then resumes to the northeast, and continues through Benin and Nigeria, before finally discharging into the Atlantic.

Located in the midst of a desert, the inland delta is a strange terrain of intertwined channels and shallow marshes that flood between September and May, receding thereafter. The river is clear all the way to the lake, which teems with over 250 species of fish, among them giant carp, puffer fish, lung fish, tiny aquarium fish such as cichlids and barbs, and fifty-eight species of catfish ranging in size from a few centimeters

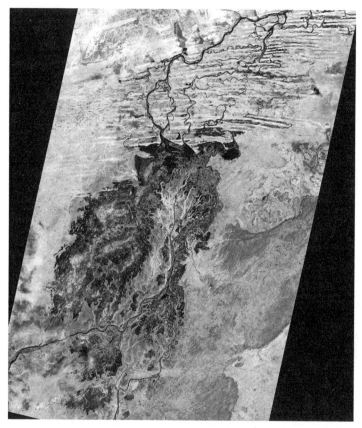

Satellite view of the Inner Niger Delta, showing the lush floodplain.
(Data available from the U.S. Geological Survey)

or inches to a few meters (several feet) in length—plus the dreaded elephant-killing fish, a small cichlid that, according to local fishermen, can lodge itself in an elephant's trunk, causing the poor animal to beat itself to death attempting to dislodge it.

Pasture lands on the lake's fringes are populated by palms and acacia trees, while the lower areas provide edible grasses that grow in water up to 3 meters (10 ft.) deep. Along with baobabs, acacias are West Africa's most iconic tree, easily recognizable by their huge umbrella-shaped crowns, dangling seed pods, and attractive yellow-white flower clusters.[1] Possibly influenced by Judeo-Christian religious beliefs, West Africans call it the "Tree of Life." (According to Old Testament lore, God is said to have commanded Moses to build his ark out of the hard wood of the acacia.)

Acacia seed pods are approximately 75 millimeters (3 in.) long and usually contain five or six seeds about 50 millimeters (2 in.) long that are brownish-black in color, turning greenish as they ripen. Because the pods are hard and practically waterproof, the seeds can be difficult to germinate. Once the pods split, it is possible to see the red stalk that attaches each seed to the pod, which resembles an umbilicus that gradually uncoils. You could say that the pod with its stalk is like a human uterus with its placenta and umbilical cord—each is a pouch that protects and nurtures the young life within.

This unusual land- and waterscape—a desert containing a long lake that turns into a river at either end—was the home of the Mali (or Keita) empire between the thirteenth and seventeenth centuries. Founded by Sundiata Keita, a warrior prince of the Keita dynasty called on to liberate his people from the rule of a rival king, the empire would extend from Timbuktu, 500 kilometers (300 mi.) east of the lake, all the way upstream to the Atlantic coast, giving the prince exclusive control of trans-Saharan commerce. Before the end of the thirteenth century his descendants were converted to Islam, but the story they tell of their beginnings—though affected as well by Islamic beliefs—incorporates a naturalistic philosophy, twinned for balance, that could only have originated in the Niger-Débo ecosphere.

Germaine Dieterlen, an anthropologist who lived for several years during the 1940s and 1950s among the Mande (who still inhabit the area today), compiled the story I recount here.[2] She wrote of their origin:

> It is quite possible that the origins and inter-relations of these peoples as asserted in the myth have no ethnic or historical reality, and the myth may well have been established for political reasons at a time when ruling groups from Mande gained control of large parts of West Africa. Nevertheless it serves to validate the relations and mutual obligations which exist among them today, and which are deeply felt and respected. The myth, therefore, expresses a widespread tradition of the unity of African peoples.[3]

The Mande myth cleverly employs the river itself to unify time (the generations) and space (the ethnic groups who live along the river).

It is said that Mangala, the ancient god of many West African people, failed in his first creative act—fashioning acacia seeds. So he attempted a more modest creation—a much smaller seed that did not require a pod. Eleusine seeds, the source of an edible weed known as goosegrass, a relative of crabgrass—a nuisance to us—are no larger than 2 millimeters (0.1 in.). To make an egg to house the seeds, he enfolded them in a larger hibiscus seed. The Keita say Mangala "made the egg of the world in *two* twin parts which were to procreate." Then he made six more seeds and identified the group of eight with the four elements and four directions, the whole of it sealed in a hibiscus seed. All were twins of opposite sex in the "Egg of God," or "placenta of the world."[4] In that same egg he placed two more pairs of twins—one male and one female; they would become the archetypes of future people.

But Pemba, the male member of one twin pair, desiring to control the creation of future people, emerged prematurely, carrying with him a torn bit of placenta. He descended through empty space and landed, his fall cushioned by the placenta fragment, which became the dried-out earth. Disappointed by his own mistake and hoping to regain entry to the egg, Pemba traveled back up to heaven. By then Mangala had already transformed what was left of the placenta into the sun. So Pemba stole a handful of male seeds from one of the clavicles of Mangala, returned to earth, and planted them in the bit of remaining placenta blood by the bank of Lake Débo, near the village of Bounan. Unfortunately, only a single eleusine seed was able to acquire enough water to germinate.

Now Pemba had sinned doubly: his theft was accompanied by incest, for he had unwittingly placed the seed in part of his own mother's womb. Thus the earth became impure, and the eleusine seed took on a red color—the way it looks today. Meanwhile, Pemba's male twin, Faro, who had achieved a full-term birth, assumed the first of several animate forms. He became twin *mannogo* fishes, one an air-breathing eel-like giant catfish (*Heterobranchus bidorsalis*), which can grow to as long as 1.5 meters (5 ft.) and a weight of 30 kg (66 lbs), representing his strength and his life; the other a smaller catfish (*Clarias senegalensis*), representing his body. They say his first essence was fishlike because a human has the shape of a fish in the mother's womb during the early stages of pregnancy. The remnant of Faro's placenta was transformed into the bright star Sirius.

Faro was also required to atone for his twin brother's sin of impurification of fertility; he was sacrificed and his body, divided into sixty pieces, was scattered through space. The fragments fell to earth where they were resurrected as trees. But Mangala brought Faro's essence back to life in heaven, gave him a human shape, and sent him down to earth on an ark made out of his celestial placenta, which had come to rest on the mountain called Kouroula in the area between Kri and Kri Koro. He renamed the place Mande, or "Son of the Person," after himself. They say Faro first became transformed into the Niger River when he came down from the cloudy sky of Mande.

Faro was accompanied by eight ancestors of humans—four pairs of male and female twins—created from his placenta. All of them, including Faro, shared a common life force that spanned both male and female sexes. Together they emerged from the ark and watched the sun rise for the first time. On the top of Kouroula they also built the first sanctuary; there they learned to pray for rain to fertilize the crops that they would soon plant. They ceased to pray only when they saw the sun and Sirius rise at the same time. (This happens in mid-July, which coincides with the beginning of the rainy season in Lake Débo.) The Keita also say that if Sirius shines brightly during the sowing, there will be "lots of rain and lots of millet."[5]

Next Pemba's female descendant was given the task of sowing the eleusine seeds, beginning on the slopes of Kouroula, while it was Faro's (male) duty to flood the path she took in order to fertilize them. They say that when he lived in heaven he walked straight, but on earth he needed to learn to walk in a sinuous way—like a water course. The series of floods that follow this flow make up Faro's body on earth, the Niger River. His head is Lake Débo, where the flooding ends; his right arm is the Bani River, which flows from the south and meets the Niger 130 kilometers (80 mi.) above the lake. His body is the area upriver from that juncture. A pair of towns, one on either side of the Niger 250 kilometers (155 mi.) farther upstream, represent his genitals; and the remainder, all the way back to the headwaters, are his single leg. (Like the fishes that swim in the Niger, the river itself has a single appendage.) As Faro follows his tortuous path toward the lake, his left and right banks alternate between male and female. But, like time, the flow of the river is also a history of the episodes of flooding experienced by Faro and his descendants.

According to the Keita, the earthly descendants of Faro, four generations associated with the four ancestor pairs who came down on the ark, were handed over the duties of sowing and guarding eleusine seeds along the banks of his body: the first generation from Kangaba to Koulikoro, the second from Koulikoro to Mopti, the third from Mopti to Akka, and the fourth to Lake Débo. As Faro taught them how to domesticate the land along the course of the Niger, they needed to be careful not to sow the impure seeds stolen by evil Pemba. The children of Faro set up their places along the banks of the river appropriate to the zones where they continue to carry out their duties. Thanks to Faro's water, the Mande people are able to grow pure eleusine seeds.

Mande history resonates today. At the beginning of the rainy season—their New Year—Mande bards representing each of the sixteen lineages that populate the banks of the Niger River participate in an all-night recitation of the creation myth told here. Today fishing rights along the Niger are divided into the areas related to the generational divisions in the story. And at the annual harvest in Kangaba, the Mande people sow a ritual field and offer a giant catfish to commemorate Faro's sacrifice in heaven. The Keita do not merely recite the story of their beginnings—they live it.

10

Tlingit Origins

Closely allied with the Tahltan and Haida, the Tlingit (People of the tide) are a semi-sedentary tribe of hunter-gatherers who live along the northwest coast of the Pacific, largely within British Columbia and Alaska. They base their living mostly on managing fisheries. So it should be no surprise that so many of their stories deal with the bounties of coastal waters and the origins of its animated denizens—including freshwater, the tides, and salmon. Tlingit tales are highly animistic, featuring interchangeable people and animal characters. They center especially on Raven, who is to the Tlingit what Coyote is to the Navajo, though he is less a creator, more a transformer—one who changes situations for the better by striving for equality and fair distribution of goods. Like Navajo Coyote, Tlingit Raven achieves his ends through trickery. Ravens thrive in north and northwest North America and are universally acknowledged to be among the most intelligent avians, well known for their technological skills. They have been described as not just large but massive, "utterly black," and having a "thick neck, shaggy throat feathers," and "a Bowie-knife-like beak."[1]

Our elders tell us he was born before the world was known—the one they called Raven, the traveling transformer. He probably came from far north in Tlingit country because he always spoke our language. This Raven was a trickster who performed miraculous feats while paddling his small canoe along the seashore of the world. Then there was no daylight—no sun, moon, or stars.

One day Raven stopped to visit some people who lived along the coastline. They told him they had heard of the one called Daylight Man, who kept many things—including daylight—imprisoned in boxes inside his house. They say that when he removed the lid of the Daylight Box his whole house lighted up. Elsewhere people couldn't move about or work because they weren't able to see their way in the perpetual darkness. Daylight Man was attended by many slaves. He also had a young daughter who lived in a corner of his big house. She would drink water out of a white bucket filled each morning by the slaves; she always looked at it closely before drinking to make sure there was nothing bad in it.

Raven conceived a plan to capture daylight and bring it into the world to share with the people. He would change himself into a cedar leaf and hide in the water. When the girl drank the water, she'd swallow Raven and he would impregnate her. Then, when the child was born, Raven would secretly get access to the Daylight Box. That was the plan; but when the girl went to drink the water she noticed a leaf floating in it, so she threw it out. Raven responded by transforming part of himself into smaller and smaller cedar leaves, until he finally was ingested. After Son of Raven was born, the young girl's parents came to adore him. They became very attached to their grandson, even though they had no idea who his father was.

One day the young toddler asked his grandfather if he would allow him to play with the moon. Naturally wanting to please the boy, Daylight Man ordered his Moon Box taken off the shelf and handed to him. The boy played with it happily but soon became bored; he began to cry, saying he now wanted to play with the sun. That was given to him and he played with it until again he became restless, so he asked for the Big Dipper and amused himself with that for a while. Next he wanted to play with the Daylight Box; but his grandfather was concerned about allowing him to do so, fearing that if the child handled it improperly it might shed too much light. Besides, the sun, moon, and stars all worked in unison with it whenever the box was moved. The boy cried and cried until his grandfather finally gave in and ordered the box containing daylight carefully removed from the shelf. Supervised by his uneasy grandfather, the boy slowly lifted the lid and gradually raised the box. Out came the light—the brighter the higher he lifted it. The old man warned "Eh, eh!" anxiously, as the boy gradually learned to balance and control the daylight.[2]

One day the Son of Raven felt confident enough to attempt the feat he'd long planned to execute. He carried the box all the way to the ceiling of Daylight Man's house, grabbing hold of the sun, moon, and stars on the way. Suddenly he flew out of the smoke hole with them. Then he let the daylight out of the box exclaiming: "Henceforth there shall be daylight, and people will be able to see and work and travel." Next he released the sun to the east, the moon to the west, and the Dipper above, exclaiming, "After dawn the sun will rise, and when it sets, night will come. People will then rest and sleep, for it will not be easy to work and travel. Then the Dipper and moon will travel and give light." Henceforth all of these things never again belonged to one man, nor were they kept locked up in one place. They were now for the use and benefit of all people.

After lighting up the world, Raven continued paddling along the coastline in his canoe. Soon he came upon starving

villagers living along the shore who had little access to game.
As he traveled farther along he noticed many different kinds of
shellfish underneath the water that were good to eat; but because the water was too deep, much of the nutritious catch was
out of reach. As he contemplated what to do about the situation, he came upon a huge man seated in the water at the shore's
edge. Raven asked him why he was sitting there. The man answered, "If I get up, the ocean will dry up." The man was actually squatting on a hole in the earth through which water
poured every time he rose. Raven told him to get up, but the
man refused. So Raven pulled him up by the hair and put a
rock under his bottom. The rock was very sharp and when the
man sat down, it hurt him and made him jump up even farther.
Raven then put a larger sharp rock beneath him and continued doing so until the big man was sitting practically upright.
Meanwhile the ocean had gone down a long way, exposing the
beach. Raven ordered him: "Henceforth you must get up twice
a day and let the sea go down, as far as it is now so that people
may obtain food from the beach. Then you will sit down again
to let the water gather and come up. If you promise to do this,
I shall not kill you." The huge man promised and that's how
the tides were created. Raven named him Tide Man. Now the
coastal people were able to find many kinds of food in abundance along the shore and they no longer starved.[3]

Now that the shoreline people had an abundant supply
of food, those who lived up the rivers that emptied there were
still starving. To help them, Raven decided he would make the
salmon that swam in the sea go up the streams. So, he took bits
of salmon roe, put a salmon egg in each, and paddled it up all
the rivers and creeks. Then he said, "The salmon will breed and
come back to these places again. These waters will be the same
as their mother's milk. The salmon must come back to them

every year. The salmon belonging to one river or creek will always return to the same stream because they were born there."[4]

Also at this time, except for rain, there was no fresh water in the world. All water tasted of salt. Raven discovered this when he visited some shoreline villagers and asked for a drink. They told him that they had only the rain from heaven, which was very scarce. Still they were able to offer him a scant cup of water, explaining: "We get a mouthful sometimes from the man who owns it." Raven asked the people the name of this man. They told him he was called Kanu'gu and they showed the transformer-trickster where he lived. Raven promptly went to his house and asked for a drink. "Water is very scarce. I can give you only a mouthful," Kanu'gu told him, as he went to a huge tank in a corner where he slept and extracted a dipper-full.[5]

Raven asked Kanu'gu if he could stay the night and he was allowed to do so. He noticed that Kanu'gu stood guard over his water tank day and night, scarcely sleeping. Still Raven managed to swipe a mouthful; he went out of the house and returned shortly with his mouth still full. When Kanu'gu asked him what he was up to, Raven swallowed a bit of the water and responded, "I am full to the mouth with the water I have drunk." When Kanu'gu asked him where he got it from, Raven responded, "I found some in a certain place. There is much of it there. You are not the only one who possesses water," as he spit out what was left in his mouth.[6]

Eager to have Raven divulge his secret, Kanu'gu invited him to stay on, help him chop wood, and do household chores. Once Raven had worked there a while, Kanu'gu became less suspicious of him and so let down his guard. One day, while his host slept in his favorite place, the trickster went outside and collected some animal excrement. He placed it by Kanu'gu's side and woke him up. "Brother-in-law, you have soiled your bed," he exclaimed. That means bad luck. Kanu'gu was ashamed and much worried by this prophecy. He didn't know what to do. "I know a medicine," Raven said. "If you take it, no bad luck will come to you. You must wash some distance away from the house with old urine. The Raven people do that and wash one another." Immediately Kanu'gu ran from the house, stripping off his clothing as he went, as Raven followed along. "You must open your eyes wide," Raven said, as he poured the urine over Kanu'gu's head. Kanu'gu was blinded for a while—just long enough for Raven to dash into the house and drink as much water from the reservoir as his belly could hold. Then he made a hole in the tank and let all the rest of the precious liquid run out. Once Kanu'gu's sight was restored and he realized he'd been duped, he ran back into the house where he confronted an empty water tank. Catching a glimpse of Raven attempting escape through the smoke hole, he grabbed pieces of charred wood from the fire and threw it at him, creating a thick cloud of rising smoke. Covered with soot, Raven managed to get away, but ever since all ravens—who used to be white—were born quite black. Finally, Raven proceeded to scatter water all over the country, saying, "Henceforth water will run here and there all over the country, and everyone will have plenty of water."[7]

Very long ago, when the world was very young, there came a great flood. It rained for days and nights and the rivers overflowed their banks; the ocean rose and inundated the land. To make matters worse, the earth was tipped and the water ran to the place where people dwelled. They fled to high ground and some climbed trees as the water rose. Others boarded hastily built rafts. Rats and mice climbed aboard and gnawed at the ropes, breaking the rafts apart. Storms and high winds blotted out the sun, moon, and the Dipper stars. All were lost from view.

Finally, after ten days, the rain stopped and the waters slowly began to recede. Survivors came down the mountains and returned to the coast. They had lost nearly everything. Then came Raven. He flew to the sky and located the sun, moon, and Dipper stars. He brought them back. He gave the people the fire and fuel he had transported from the dry mountaintops. Finally, he cured the earth from tipping. It seems the earth was much lighter in those days. It rolled up and down, displacing the ocean. So water would rush to one place and stay for a while. Then the earth would tip, and the water would rush back again. To make the earth secure and steady, Raven flew to the far north and gathered a huge chunk of ice from the great glaciers in high mountains and placed it on the earth to weigh it down and prevent it from tipping. Ever since then, the earth rumbles and shakes once in a while, but otherwise it's been steady and floods are no more.

PART THREE

CAVES

Except for their flatness, the treeless, desert landscape of the Nullarbor Plain of southwest Australia and the tropical jungles of Mexico's Yucatán peninsula could not look more different. But these two places, located on opposite sides of the globe, have something else in common. Their limestone topographies are honeycombed with giant, sinuous caves that form the backdrop for climactic scenes in creation stories passed down to contemporary dwellers.

Dreamtime stories told by Aboriginal Australians feature a female sun deity who dives into the caves and awakens the sleeping spirits of the first world creatures—insects, snakes, and birds—trusting they will live in harmony on the surface of the world above. In the ancient Maya domain Xibalba (Place of fear) is the palatial cavern-temple where the lords of the underworld reside. They are the bearers of all forms of pestilence and misfortune and stand ready to inflict their evils on anyone molded by the androgynous creator whom the people call "Maker-Modeler." But Hero Twins sent from above penetrate the underworld entrance, fending off obstacles set up to thwart their ultimate confrontation with the forces of evil. Their other enemy is time, for they must emerge victorious over the evil lords before the first dawn and the sowing of life on earth.

Descendants of the Inca of Peru, who also live in a landscape riddled with caves, tell the story of the supreme rich one, their first king, who emerged from a cave that led from Lake Titicaca, where the creator god Viracocha fashioned him out of clay that had not yet hardened into solid earth, to the place where the Inca would build the capital of their powerful empire.

The magical power of transformation—the ability to shift shape and form—emerges once again as a recurrent element in these stories: human is transformed to bird in the Inca story, while in the Maya tale the Twins are endowed with the extraordinary ability to kill, then bring themselves back from the dead—a power they put to good use in tricking the evil lords into a one-way trip. In the Aboriginal myth the first creatures, dissatisfied with who they are, have the power to transform themselves, from tiny fish to frogs and mice to bats. Whether you live above or below ground, self-satisfaction can often be difficult to achieve.

To understand where this sort of transformative imagery might come from in the natural world, take a close look at a downed tree in the woods. From one perspective it looks like a tree, but from another it blends into an amorphous, rotting mass on the forest floor. Probe that dark matter and you might find a tiny sprout nurtured by the rich surroundings. What once was alive returns again to life.

11

A Dreamtime Creation from Southwest Australia

Any mythic map of Australia is sure to reveal the most important characters tied in some way to the landscape.[1] So wrote one mythologist of the Aboriginal Australian people. Though the myths are diverse, much of what they have to say connects directly with what geographers and geologists have discovered about changes in the landscape that have taken place over thousands of years: fertile areas that once occupied present-day deserts, places now submerged that once formed the coastline along the Great Barrier Reef, and dormant volcanoes. In a sense, Aboriginal myths ring true. The landscape was created and transformed in what indigenous storytellers call "Dreamtime"—a time out of time, when heroic, supernatural ancestors played an active role in creating sacred places, people, animals, plants, laws, and customs. Dreamtime is the source of all Aboriginal knowledge and laws of existence.

This story was originally told by a Karraru woman from the southwest coast of Australia. It takes place on Nullarbor Plain, a 600 kilometer (400 mi.)–long tableland devoid of veg-

etation. Geologists have determined that it was once an ancient limestone seabed pockmarked with sinkholes and pock-
eted with sinuous caves—among the largest water-filled caves
in the world.[2]

The darkness that covered the earth was cold, silent, still, and
everywhere. It enveloped the mountains, the valleys, and the
caves of Nullarbor. In the deepest of caverns at the place called
Killa-wilpa-nina lived the beautiful goddess Karraru.[3] There
she slept at night and traveled to the east to begin the morning.
She opened her eyes, took a deep breath, and caused the darkness to disappear. Then she went up into the sky and traveled
over the barren landscape from east to west. In her footsteps
the face of the earth suddenly sprouted grass, trees, and plants.
Then she descended under the ground and returned to Killa-
wilpa-nina. Next day she repeated her journey, diverging a bit
northward along her course. After many more days of traveling farther north Karraru began to pursue a more southerly
course, returning after a year of days back to where she had
begun. All the while plants and animals continued to stream
out of each of her footsteps until the landscape from far north
to south was covered with living things.

Once she had prepared the earth, Karraru descended
deep into the caves, bringing with her light and warmth. She
melted the solid ice that covered the underworld. There she
woke the sleeping spirits of the insects of every color and size
and bid them go forth into the upper world to make it more
beautiful. Next she brought up the snakes and lizards; then all
kinds of animals emerged out of holes in the ground and began
to walk over the landscape. Into the rivers that issued out of
the melted ice in the caverns she placed fish of all kinds, great
and small. Pleased with her work, Karraru flew back to the
verdant landscape of Nullarbor. She gave the creatures she had

awakened the power to be themselves as they wished, trusting all would live together in harmony—but this did not happen.

After a while some of the furry animals became jealous of the birds because they possessed the ability to fly. Some fish complained because they didn't get as much sunshine as the other animals. These creatures just didn't like who they were. Because at that time they had the power to become who they wished, they decided to change their shapes. Some mice transformed themselves into birds without feathers. Squirrels and foxes did the same. Tiny fish changed into frogs. Birds who gave themselves bigger eyes so they could hunt at night were forced to spend the bright light of day in dark caves. Strange animals—kangaroos, wombats, and koalas, and a creature with a bill like a duck and a tail like a beaver—began to take over the landscape. When the Sun Goddess saw how her creations were behaving, she brought forth two children—the morning star and the moon. They gave birth to two children and sent them to earth. They would become our ancestors and help guide the animals. They would be given the gift of intelligence and they would be wise enough never to want to change their shape. But how would this gift come?

The Sun Goddess commanded the winds to take this new intelligence to all parts of earth. As it passed over the north, east, south, and west, the winds set the ocean waters into huge roiling billows. Lightning flashed—it struck the mountains and hurled rocks into the wind. Kangaroo, wombat, emu—all fled into the caves as the torrential rains flooded the land. Birds, lizards, and insects alike trembled, hiding away in the ensuing darkness. Next morning the sun rose and all seemed quiet. No living creature dared emerge from hiding. Finally a goanna (giant lizard) peeked out the cave entrance. "What have you seen?," asked the eagle-hawk anxiously. "I saw a form a little larger than the kangaroo. His eyes were not so big as the goannas but, oh, they were so bright!"[4] Finally, the animals screwed up enough courage to brave a look. Then the two-legged creatures approached the entrance to the cave and offered the animals food for their families, beckoning them to venture above and receive the gift of intelligence. They assembled all together—people and animals—on a hilltop in the middle of the plain they had selected. There they waited, and after a while the sharp-eyed eagle-hawk spotted a pillar of swirling dust to the north, then another to the west, moving toward them. A third pillar followed from the south, then one from the east. The four dust pillars converged and descended to the hilltop. A thunderbolt shot out of the screaming wind and the voice of the goddess sounded a message of love over their heads, as she transferred her intelligence to the humans. She decreed that they must take care of and live in harmony with all the creatures of the world. Then the Sun Goddess continued on her journey from east to west every day, moving north to south and back again over the eons, promising never again to stop.[5]

12

An Underworld Battle and the Maya Dawn of Life

We think of the horizon as the line of demarcation between things terrestrial (geographical or geological) and celestial (meteorological and astronomical), but the Maya of Yucatán, who speak of "all the sky-earth," recognize no such boundary. Maya cosmic myths like the *Popol Vuh* (Council book) may strike us as amusing stories, but behind the terrestrial and celestial alliances mentioned in their story of creation lie real people asking the kinds of questions we no longer tend to ask when we look outward and upward.[1] What is the origin of gender and sex? Where does fertility—or for that matter any power—come from? Where do we go when we die? How can we know what will happen to us in the future? Perhaps to keep them secret from their Spanish conquerors, answers to many of their inquiries in the narrative are encoded in the metaphor of visible planetary characteristics and changes; for example, descent and resurrection (particularly for Mercury and Venus, the planets seen closest to the sun), and dyadic and triadic bonds (among the sun, moon, and Venus). From contemporary studies of their writings, it is clear that the Maya possessed a vast and precise knowledge of astronomy. The version of the *Popol Vuh* I have chosen here is adapted from Dennis Tedlock's account, with running commentary by Andrs Xiloj, one of the lineage's spiritual leaders from highland Guatemala.[2]

The Maya were motivated not by a desire to express the workings of nature in terms of inert mathematical equations but rather by the need to know how to mediate an alliance between the inherent power within the universe and humankind in a way that would enhance human well-being. Their goal was to bring the knowledge of the cosmos to human action. For the Maya, telling stories about everyday affairs during particular periods of change in the natural world offered a logical way both to embellish life and to lend a meaningful structure to time, with which they were clearly obsessed.[3] The names of most of the characters in the *Popol Vuh*—for example, One and Seven Death, and Hunahpu (One Lord)—are dates in their 260-day sacred round. Imagine your birthday serving as your name and you'll get the idea. In some instances, especially in highly structured societies like the Classic Maya (200–900 CE), the relationship between people and the natural world became formalized through the ruling class. Thus we discover elements of the *Popol Vuh* story in the monumental inscriptions and other artistic renderings in their ruined cities, where carved stone effigies depict young rulers as sprouting corn plants.[4]

That maize should lie at the heart of creation made good sense to the Maya: you are what you eat, and maize agriculture is the lifeblood of Maya culture. The sowing and dawning of the world—the sowing of seeds in the earth, which will dawn when they have sprouted, as well as the sowing of the sun, moon, and stars destined to illuminate the sky—is likened to the germination of human beings in the womb, destined to be born into the world.

There are no rivers in Mayaland. The karst topography of the Yucatán heartland is riddled with natural sinkholes called cenotes, pits that form where groundwater dissolves the limestone bedrock. More than six thousand cenotes are known in the Yucatán peninsula, the largest penetrating to depths of more than 100 meters (350 ft.) and connecting with extensive underwater cave systems. Contemporary Maya still make offerings at many ancient sites containing cenotes. Cenotes and caves prompted the Maya to speculate about the unknown world that lay beneath their feet and how it connects with the world above, home of the androgynous heavenly creator deity—the one they called Maker-Modeler, and the Hero Twins sent to battle the sinister forces of death and disease named One and Seven Death, who inhabit the cave world below. At stake is the answer to the question: who will tend the world in between—the surface of the earth—once the sun rises?

The climactic scene takes place underground in a region called Xibalba, or Place of Fear, which is accessible via two aboveground passages. (Cave systems containing artifacts, stone temples, and human bones discovered at various archaeological sites in Guatemala and Mexico are thought to have been Maya entrances to the underworld.) The Hero Twins follow one of the perilous routes to the underworld, where they confront rivers of blood and pus, and dark houses filled with bats, before finally arriving at the palace of One and Seven Death. There the ultimate pre-creation battle of wits takes place.

As in a number of creation stories we've encountered, the *Popol Vuh* at the very outset gives readers a sense of how hard it is to manage creation. After all, the gods aren't perfect.

Mayas climbing down into a limestone sinkhole, called a cenote, at Bolonchén, Yucatán. (Frederick Catherwood, *Mayas descend into the cenote at Bolonchén, Yucatán*, London, 1843)

Creation was a great performance—a long drama to bring about the emergence of "all the sky-earth":

> by the Maker, Modeler,
> mother-father of life, of humankind,
> giver of breath, giver of heart,
> bearer, upbringer in the light that lasts
> of those born in the light, begotten in the light;
> worrier, knower of everything, whatever there is:
> sky-earth, lake-sea.[5]

In the beginning there was not a single human, animal, fish, or tree; no cave, canyon, meadow, or forest. There was only the sky above and the sea below. Nothing moved, nothing stirred. Then the Maker-Modeler, the Mother-Father, talked about how to create the sowing and dawning. They talked with the other gods—with Sovereign Plumed Serpent, with Thunderbolt Hurricane, with Heart of Sky. First they decided to create it by word—speaking the words: "Earth, let it be this way, think about it"—and the mountains rose from the water, separated from the water, and formed the streams and valleys. Thus they had no trouble creating animals—deer, birds, pumas and jaguars, rattlesnakes and fer-de-lances.[6]

Talk to each other in your own languages, the gods commanded the newly formed guardians of the bush. "Name now our names," said the gods. "We are your mother-father; speak, pray to us, keep our days." But the animals only squawked and chattered and howled. "It hasn't turned out well," said the Maker-Modeler, Bearer-Begetter, Mother-Father. You will have to be transformed, they told the animals: "What you feed on, what you eat, the places where you sleep, the places where you stay, whatever is yours will remain in the canyons, the forests." And you must "let your flesh be eaten" as your service, by those we have yet to create who will keep our days. Now they needed to create people to carry out the demanding task of tending to their new environment. But the gods became anxious, for though there was yet no sun, the light of dawn had already begun to appear in the east.[7]

So the gods tried creating again, saying, "The time for the planting and dawning is nearing. For this, we must make a provider and a nurturer. How else can we be invoked and remembered on the face of the earth?"[8] This time the Mother-Father tried working with earth and mud. They molded a body, but it wouldn't hold together. Its head wouldn't turn and it had a lopsided face. It talked but its speech made no sense. Realizing their failure, they gave up and let it melt into a lifeless blob.

Next they tried their hand at carpentry. They made wood carvings—manikins with sticks for arms and legs. They gouged out mouths in their heads that talked. The wooden creatures even multiplied; they had sons and daughters. But they had no blood, no lymph, no fat—their faces were crusty and dried out. Worst of all, "there was nothing in their hearts and nothing in their minds."[9] They had no memory of who made them. They just walked around aimlessly. So the gods sent a great flood to wash them away.

Now time was running short and things began to get more tense. The sun was about to dawn and the gods had failed to create creatures who could tend to things on earth. And so from the sky the gods sent the Hero Twins, Hunahpu and Xbalanque (One Lord and Seven Lord). Once they had acquired some experience combating bad things above the surface of the world, they set out in haste to conquer evil forces attempting to emerge from the underworld so that the world stage would be set for the great dawning.

The twins descended into Xibalba at the entrance where the dark Great Rift of the Milky Way meets the eastern horizon.

Down they went, successively combating the evils in pitch-black Dark House, Jaguar House—a place full of brawling jaguars—and a hail-filled Cold House. Finally they arrived at the underworld lair of the evil Lords of Xibalba—Blood Gatherer, Bloody Teeth, Jaundice Master, Pus Master, Scab Master, and Bone Scepter, and their leaders One and Seven Death—bearers of maladies and disease, whose only concern was to make life unbearable for any race that would come to inhabit the earth once the sun rose. From the messengers they sent to the world above, these evil lords had heard of the twins' reputation for being not only cunning and clever, but also superlative dancers and entertainers.

"Who are these two vagabonds? Are they really such a delight? And is their dancing really that pretty?" asked the one named One Death, head of all Underworld Lords. "They do everything!," was the response. But once the twins came into their presence, looking quite unmajestic and dressed only in tattered rags, the lords looked puzzled. They wanted to be entertained. To please them, the boys began with a few dances. They danced the Weasel, then they danced the Whippoorwill and the Armadillo. Looking bored, the Xibalbans demanded a magical performance: "Sacrifice my dog, [and] then bring him back to life again," charged one of the lords. So they sacrificed the dog and he came back to life. He looked really happy when he came back to life—even wagged his tail. Bet you can't kill a person by making a sacrifice without death, challenged One Death, upping the ante: "Do it to yourselves. Let's see it . . . that's the dance we really want from you!" Without hesitating, Hunahpu took hold of brother Xbalanque and spread out his legs and arms on a rounded stone altar. Then he grabbed his lightning-striking ax. He chopped off his brother's head and the lords watched it roll away. Then he dug out his brother's heart, wrapped it in a leaf and held it aloft. Seeing this, the

Xibalbans went crazy with delight. "Get up!," said Hunahpu, looking down at his brother's limp remains; whereupon Xbalanque instantaneously returned to life. He even danced to prove his new vitality.[10]

One and Seven Death marveled at the spectacle and all the Lords of the Underworld danced in a crazed frenzy. "Do it to us! Sacrifice us!" and "Sacrifice both of us!," they demanded. The Lords of the Underworld were enthralled with longing, yearning to know what it would feel like to die and magically come back to life. "What is death to you?," retorted the twins. "And aren't we making you happy, along with the vassals of your domain?"[11] Eagerly One Death stepped up. He was first to be sacrificed. And when he was killed, Seven Death went next. Except the Hero Twins didn't bring them back to life. When the lesser lords saw what happened, they became confused and perplexed. A few followed suit and submitted to sacrifice. Others realized the clever twins had tricked them. They tearfully pleaded with the victors to take pity on them. The remainder of the underworld inhabitants were taken to a great canyon and piled up in a deep abyss. Like countless ants they tumbled down into a huge cave, bent low in surrender, meek and still tearful. Such was the defeat of the rulers of Xibalba. And so the boys accomplished the wonders of self-transformation.

And this was the punishment addressed to the defeated lords by their conquerors: From this day forward, your gifts of bringing pestilence upon the world will no longer be great. You, Scab Master, the only scabs you will cause will be "reduced to scabrous nodules of tree sap." And you, Blood Gatherer, "You will only feed on the creatures of the meadows and clearings."[12] Such was the disappearance of so many of the horrible diseases once thought destined to plague the world.

Finally, the world stage was set for the successful creation of people—the ones fit to say the names of their mother-father creators. These were the ingredients they worked with. First there was water for blood. Next there was corn for flesh—yellow corn, white corn—the gods ground them together. The grease from their hands that they used to mold them became human fat. It was by these staples alone that the hands of gods made humanity. They made four of them, and so divided the humans up into lineages who would be the first fathers of all subsequent people. The gods watched and listened to what they had created and they saw that the people talked; they looked; they walked; they became knowledgeable. Then the gods thanked their Hero Twin offspring for helping put the world in order by giving the people a safe place, just as the sun was now about to rise. And so the two boys ascended. And when it finally became light on the face of the earth, they were there in the sky, the sun belonging to one, the moon to the other.

13

Inca Ancestors Emerge

Stretching along the Andes from Ecuador to southern Argentina, the Inca empire at the time of Columbus's arrival was the largest in the New World. (The Aztec empire in Central Mexico was second.) It had coalesced in the mid-fifteenth century, when the ruler Túpac Inca Yupanqui undertook a program of military expansion at the behest of his ancient ancestors, who, so the story goes, had emerged from a cave near where he would found his capital, Tahuantinsuyu.

The landscape of Tahuantinsuyu (Realm of the Four Parts), the location of today's Cusco, Peru, is riddled with caves, many of which suit the exit point in the myth, depending on who tells the story. Ethnic groups in the vicinity of any of them would certainly be gratified to learn that the favored locale of their beginnings lay in their own backyard.

In the beginning all lay in darkness. Out of a lake near Tiahuanaco, high in the mountains in the direction named Collasuyu, emerged the god Viracocha. He created the sun god Inti, along with the moon Mama Quilla, his sister-wife. She has dark spots on her face because her husband threw ashes on her countenance out of jealousy over her brightness. Inti and Mama Quilla in turn birthed the first humans. Inti sent his most precious children, Ayar Manco (Son of the Sun) and his sister-wife Mama Ocllo (Daughter of the Moon), accompanied by three brother-sister pairs, into a cave that would lead via a long underground passageway to an exit at a sacred cave called Tambo Toco (House of Windows) in Pacaritambo (Inn of Dawn). There were three openings in the cave, and Ayar Manco and his wife emerged from the middle one. Upon exiting the sacred cave, Ayar Manco proceeded to pierce the ground with the golden staff given him by Inti in order to find the place where it would penetrate, thus rendering it fertile for planting the first maize. At that place he would become the first ruler. And from there, with the help of the stone warriors (*pururaucas*), the people of the sun would civilize and unite all the races of the world, reigning over them in peace forever.[1]

But the ancestors' trip was not uneventful, for they needed to contend with rival kin groups, who also had found their way through the underground passageway from the lake to the sacred cave and emerged from adjacent windows. They too needed a place to settle. They also confronted problems within their own kin group. Brother Ayar Cachi was particularly unruly, using his sling to demolish hills, causing rocks and dust to fly up into the sky. To get rid of him, Ayar Manco decided to send him back to the Tambo Toco cave to retrieve some sacred objects he said he had mistakenly left behind, among them a golden cup, a packet of seeds, and a miniature effigy of a llama—a sign of nobility. Along with his brother he sent a man from one of the tribes allied with the ancestors, whom Ayar Manco had persuaded to get rid of his nuisance brother. When the pair arrived at Tambo Toco, Ayar Cachi entered the cave in search of the articles. Promptly his companion sealed the cave entrance for all time with a huge boulder.

Once Ayar Manco and his clan arrived at the peak of the

Inca worship their ancestors at the cave of Tambo Toco. (Felipe Guaman Poma de Ayala, *El Primer Nueva Corónica y buen gobierno por Felipe Guaman Poma de Ayala.* Courtesy of Siglo XXI Editores)

mountain called Huanacauri, they viewed for the first time the valley that would become their home. They knew this was the place when Ayar Manco saw the sign of the rainbow—and when, upon his descent, he was able to sink the entire golden shaft into the earth.

Now brother Ayar Uchu spread out a pair of wings and flew from the mountaintop all the way up to heaven. He returned and told of a conversation with the sun, who decreed that hereinafter Ayar Manco would be Manco Cápac (Supreme Rich One). His work finished, Ayar Uchu immediately turned himself to stone. And so Manco Cápac domesticated the landscape by planting the first maize field. Thereafter the ancestors of the Inca, led by their first king, were worshipped at Tambo Toco, which became an important place of pilgrimage.[2]

PART FOUR

ISLANDS

If you happen to live on an island in the middle of a vast ocean, geology matters—especially if you want to know how your home got there. If an active volcano is nearby, you might imagine that your place formed when rocks were thrown down from above, while if you inhabit a quiescent terrain gradually uplifted by tectonic forces, you might find a story of your island being dredged up from the bottom of the sea more believable. Witnessing earth suddenly emerging from the sea is not uncommon in Polynesian waters, especially where tectonic plates come in contact. On occasion massive sheets of floating pumice resulting from underwater volcanic eruptions have been sighted. In Hawaii, the trickster god Maui pulled the islands up from the ocean with a magic fishhook. Parent myths from the Polynesian world feature battles among an animated family of nature's forces—worst of all the storm that constantly threatens defenseless people who live close to the sea.

Biology plays a major role in the continuity of creation narratives among the Dobu islanders of the southeast Asian archipelago. They assemble annually at a full moon to gather masses of worms that emerge from the sea, on the surface of which they deposit their genital product. They say their ancestors came from a world where all forms of life shifted shapes instantaneously from one to another—and they had a brilliant solution to the chicken-egg problem. In the Shinto creation myth from Japan, "How Our Islands Were Made," the world originally looked like an egg. Most of the creative action is undertaken by a male deity angry over having bequeathed his wife evil children. It all takes place on Ahaji (Unsatisfactory island), a place still known for its dangerous tides, whirlpools, and earthquakes.

A final pair of island-related stories comes from the Haudenosaunee (Iroquois) and the Cherokee of the northern and southern Appalachians, respectively. While we would not think of their turf as island locations, a look at the geography of the northeastern United States and eastern Canada shows a world bordered on all sides by water. Though the Cherokee myth, which imagines a curious inverted world beneath our feet, focuses on mountain making—by a giant bird flapping its wings—it and the Hawaiian myth are among many that were imported via cultural contact.

14

A Creation Story
from Polynesia

The earth's surface is 78 percent water, and the thousand tiny islands that make up Polynesia in the central and southern Pacific Ocean add up to only 2 percent of the land's share—provided you do not count New Zealand, which is located at its extreme southwestern edge. So it is not surprising to find that the tension between forces of land and water emerges as a key theme in Polynesian tales of how the world the islanders experience was created. From Hawaii in the north to Easter Island in the southeast, the creation stories resemble the one I have chosen to retell here. It features a battle of highly personified forces of nature born out of the female earth and male sky, who were eternally united until the children of creation pried their parents apart and the two were let loose in the emerging daylight. These forces include the forest and products of the land. But the most threatening character, who takes a leading role, is the Storm. Posing a profound threat to civilization trying to make a go of it in the midst of a vast ocean, the Storm eternally eats away at the precious edges of the landscape, causing the level of the sea to rise.

He becomes especially dangerous when he takes the form of extreme weather events, such as a hurricane. The embattled people must take on his fiercest fighting form to defend their dwindling landscape and allow the body of mother earth to continue to nourish her offspring.

Place:
A tiny island in the middle of the south Pacific Ocean.
Time:
Before the world came to be as we know it.
Cast of characters:
Rangí—Heaven
Papá—Earth
Children of Rangí and Papá:
> Tané—Keeper of the forest and all that
> resides there
> Tawhiri—Ruler of the wind and storms
> Rongo—Father of all cultivated foods
> Tangaroa—In charge of fish and reptiles
> Haumia—Ruler of wild foods
> Tū-matauenga—God and father of fierce
> human beings

There was darkness everywhere because these two, Father Rangí and Mother Papá, clung tightly together. The children they begat lay wedged between their bodies, never knowing there could be a difference between light and dark. As an old *karakia* (Maori incantation) taught them: "There was darkness from the first division of time, to the tenth, to the hundredth, to the thousandth." Worn out by these cramped conditions, the children of Rangí and Papá puzzled over what to do with their clingy parents. Should they kill them, or just pry them apart? Tū-matauenga, fiercest of all the sons, exhorted, "It is well, let us slay them." Brother Tané disagreed: "Nay, not so. It is better to rend them apart, and to let Rangí stand far above us, and Papá lie beneath our feet." All the brothers consented with the exception of Tawhiri, who dissented because he feared his kingdom would be overthrown by such a disruption.[1]

The plan now in place, Rongo stepped forth and volunteered to pry his parents apart from their eternal embrace. Wedging himself between them he pushed up, but he couldn't summon enough strength to budge the pair. Next Tangaroa arose to give it a try. He too failed, as did Haumia and Tū-matauenga. Now it was Tané's turn. The forest deity struggled, pushing up with his arms and down with his legs, also to no avail. Finally he flipped over and planted his head against Papá, his feet raised up against Rangí. He took a deep breath and strained his back and limbs, pushing and pushing in a mighty effort. His parents groaned loudly, "Why commit so dark a crime as to slay us, to rend us, your parents, apart?," as they slowly relented and began to separate. Tané didn't pause—he pressed Papá beneath him at the same time thrusting Rangí far, far above him. As the chant of the karakia says: "It was the fierce thrusting of Tané which tore the heaven from the earth, so that they were rent apart, and darkness was made manifest, and light made manifest also."[2]

Now the forces allied with heaven exacted revenge for what Rangí's children did to him. Tawhiri, especially, remained angry with his brothers for going against his wishes. He became consumed by a deep desire to wage war on them. He decided to forsake his mother and follow his father into the now boundless skies. There he took counsel with Rangí and raised a brood of allied forces that came to be known as the mighty winds. He dispatched one of them to the east, another to the west, one to the north, and one to the south. Then he sent forth an army of other children—Fierce Squall, Whirlwind,

Dense Cloud, Hurricane Announcer Cloud, Fiery Black Cloud, Glowing Red Light Cloud, Wildly Drifting Cloud, Thunderstorm Cloud, and Hurriedly Flying Cloud.[3] Allied by his militant forces, Tawhiri and his family constantly menaced the tiny islands. Poor Tané struggled to withstand the powerful breath of Tawhiri. His great trees were snapped off at the base, their branches splintered and shattered, their fruits strewn across the landscape and left to rot.

Next Tawhiri swept down on the sea. Huge whirlpools frightened brother Tangaroa, who fled to the deepest part of the ocean desperately seeking safety for his offspring, the fish, and the reptiles. What shall we do? Where can we go? the children worried. Let us fly inland, said the reptiles. We'd better head for the deep sea, responded the fish. The karakia says that this was called the great separation of the children of Tangaroa, who became very upset over the children who deserted him and sought refuge in the domain of Tané. That's why, ever since, he has waged war against his brother. And it's also why Tané felt the need to supply his brother Tū-matauenga's children with canoes, spears, fishhooks made from his trees, and nets woven from his fibrous plants—so that they may destroy Tangaroa's offspring. In return, Tangaroa swallowed up Tané's children by overwhelming their canoes with wave swells and wasting away the island shores with unending lapping, sapping waves.

Now Tawhiri turned to attack his brothers Rongo and Haumia. But Papá came to their defense. She caught them up and hid them in a safe place where they and their children and grandchildren couldn't be found. Then Tawhiri rushed against Tū-matauenga to challenge him strength versus strength—a battle of the two strongest brothers. Tawhiri applied all his force, but to no avail as Tū-matauenga repulsed him. He stood erect and unshaken on the breast of his mother Papá until the hearts of father Rangí and son Tawhiri finally became quieted.

Still, Tū-matauenga continued to brood over the cowardly way his brothers had acted, leaving him alone to show his courage. He began by seeking revenge on Tané. He collected fibrous blades from his brother's *whanake* tree.[4] He split the blades and twisted them into nooses to make snares. He hid them about the forest so that Tané's children would never be able to move about or fly safely. To punish Tangaroa, who had also deserted him in combat, Tū-matauenga cut many blades of flax, split them in strips, and knotted together some nets. Dragging them through the water, he hauled many of the children of Tangaroa ashore. Finally, Tū-matauenga dealt with Rongo and Haumia. He collected some of the sturdiest whanake leaves and shaped them into digging implements; he plaited baskets; he dug in the earth and pulled up all kinds of plants with edible roots and left them to wither in the sun.

Having defeated his brothers, Tū-matauenga and his future children—fierce men—would be left to fight alone against Tawhiri. Ever after, the storm would become the eternal enemy of man, unceasingly attacking him with hurricanes, attempting to destroy him by sea and by land.

Let's not forget that it was the bursting forth of the wrathful fury of Tawhiri against his brothers that started it all. That's what caused the disappearance of so much of the dry land, for it was during that contest that a great part of Papá got submerged. Only a small portion of our mother now remains above the sea. From that time clear light has increased upon the earth, and all the beings hidden between Rangí and Papá before they were separated have now multiplied on the earth. Though the first beings born of Rangí and Papá were not human, the children of Tū-matauenga have come to bear the likeness of people.

As for Rangí and Papá, they remain separated—but their love of one another continues. If you pay close attention you can hear the soft, warm sighs of her loving bosom still rising up to him, ascending from the wooded mountains and valleys. We call them mists. And Rangí, as he mourns through the long nights over being separated from his loved one, lets fall frequent tears upon Papá's bosom. We call them dewdrops.

15

How Maui Dredged Up the Hawaiian Islands

O Lono! Lono! Lonokaeho!
Lonokulani, ali'i of Kauluonana,
Here are canoes, come aboard,
Return with us to live in green-backed Hawai'i,
A land discovered in the ocean,
Thrown up amid the waves,
From the very depths of Kanaloa,
The white coral jagged in the water
Caught on the hook of the fisherman
The great fisherman of Kapa'ahu
The great fisherman of Kapuhe'euanu'u-la
When the canoes land, come aboard,
Sail to rule Hawai'i, an island, Hawai'i is an island,
Hawai'i is an island
For Lonokaeho to live in.

The Pacific islands—were they fished up from below or thrown down from above? The "fished up" explanation appears in stories from the southern region of Samoa, Tonga, and French

Polynesia, which, except for Samoa, are largely made of limestone and were the earliest to be occupied. There shallow submarine volcanoes were known to have been active during human occupation, and likely inspired such stories. Other fishing-up stories may recollect seismic uplift events accompanied by earthquakes of the kind that commonly occur at plate boundaries in the southwest Pacific. The throwing-down myths originate in places, especially in the western parts of Polynesia, where volcanoes have been observed to erupt; thus the scene in one story from the Marshall Islands that refers to earth spilling out of a basket carried by the trickster deity Etao.

Maui is another trickster folk hero whose exploits are legion in Polynesian myths that diffused northward to the later-occupied Hawaiian Islands. Most famous among them is the story of how he fished up from the depths of the Pacific the islands we know today.[1]

Maui loved to fish in the coral reefs below Mount Haleakalā. Once it was all that existed above the water's surface. His older brothers often teased him because he only rarely caught a fish. What the brothers didn't know was that Maui possessed a magical fishhook he made out of the jawbone of a divine ancestor given him by his grandmother—and kept secret from everyone.

One day Maui decided to get even with his brothers by playing a trick on them. He invited them on a fishing trip in his canoe. He instructed his brothers to paddle and not look behind them lest the expedition should fail. They agreed, and Maui let out his line until the magical hook caught the ocean bottom. "Paddle as hard as you can," he told his brothers. "Looks like I've got a huge fish." As they did, Maui hauled up a large island—the one later named after him. "Keep pulling and don't turn around," he instructed them. He pulled up an even bigger island—Hawaii. Then another, Oahu; then Kauai; then Lanai;

Satellite photo of the Hawaiian Islands. Were they originally fished up from the sea? (Courtesy of Jacques Descloitres, MODIS Land Rapid Response Team at NASA GSFC, NASA Earth Observatory)

then Molokai, Niihau, Kahoolawe, and Nihoa. Suddenly a bailing gourd appeared on the water. Maui grabbed hold of it and placed it next to him. The gourd transformed into a beautiful water goddess. "Don't turn around," he continued; but the brothers could resist no longer. As they turned to gaze at the beautiful goddess, the line suddenly went slack—breaking the spell. The islands, which were about to coalesce, slipped partway back into the sea. That's why Hawaii is a chain of islands instead of a single large land mass.

In a second version of the story, a struggling fish is hauled up. The fish lunges downward, rises and rushes down again. As the brothers help handle it, the head of the fish emerges above the waves and changes into a land mass. But it continues to struggle and thrash about, until it breaks off in front, remaining smoothly rounded in the back and narrow in the middle. The underside rolls above the water and the upper side slides beneath as Maui chants about the overturned fish—which becomes the land Havaiki (Hawaii).[2]

In a Maori version of the myth, Maui baits his hook with blood from his nose. Casting the line into the sea, he instantly hauls up a great fish. As the greedy brothers randomly hack it up, hewing out of it great chunks to get their share, the fish-become-island assumes its present shape: a bumpy terrain of mountains and valleys, deep lakes and high cliffs—the North Island of New Zealand. They say if you look closely at a map of it you can still see the outline of the curved body of a fish: the tail is at the north, the head at the south, and the fins thrust outward on either side.

In Tonga and Samoa, Tangaloa—we remember him as Tangaroa in the Polynesian creation story—does the fishing. He hooks a huge stone, raises it to the surface, and offers it to his son, Tuli, the bird deity, as a place to live. But when Tuli goes to claim it, he discovers that waves and swells have inundated much of its surface, requiring him to hop from one part of exposed land to another to keep from getting his feet wet by the continually pounding surf. Upset by this he complains to his father, who solves the problem by taking hold of the mighty fishhook himself and raising the land to its current level.[3]

16

Dobu Islanders and
Palolo Worms

If the magic could be recovered, men would fly again in their
canoes, they could rejuvenate, defy ogres and perform the many
heroic deeds they did in ancient times.

—*B. Malinowski,* Argonauts of the Western Pacific

What if you inhabited a world where the contours of the sky,
ocean, land, and mountains were not fixed—a place where
plants and animals come out of the ground, slough off their
skins, and change shapes, where elephants become mice, rocks
become ships, people become trees—and back again? One anthropologist who spent quite a bit of time studying the Dobu
has suggested that they believe that all sorts of events happened in the ancient past that no longer happen, including
that people back then were endowed with powers that present-
day people and their historical ancestors no longer have.[1]

The Dobu live on a tiny, three-by-five kilometer (two-by-
three mile) island covered by rainforest, off the coast of southern Papua New Guinea. The island, the remnants of a long-

extinct volcano, is exactly what they say their world used to be like. The original Dobu battled monsoons alternating with drought, managing to carve out productive private gardens where a husband and a wife grew yams, along with taro (a starchy root vegetable) and sugarcane. What took place during this long-ago creation time, they say, has given us the world we know today.

The Dobu think of nature and culture as "coextensive," with the first human beings emerging "already equipped with their ornaments, trinkets, gardens, cooking vessels, and language, in the guise of certain magical incantations . . . springing from the ground along with these first ancestors."[2] Their very language speaks of it; for example, *manua* means bird and *emanua* means to change into a bird; *gurewa* means rock and *egurewa* means to become a rock by metamorphosis; *nid* means person and *emanua nidi* means a human who changed into a bird. Creation *is* metamorphosis.

How were the islands made? Where did the sea come from? And the fish that swim in it? Why do some fish, like sharks, eat people? Why does the sea taste bitter? And how did fish end up in the crater lake at the top of Mount Solomanaki, so high above the sea? Dobu creation stories deal with all these pressing environmental questions in ways that may make little sense to us. And they relate it all to the here and now by annually scanning the waters for the appearance of, believe it or not, a worm.

The beginning of time for the Dobu occurred only four generations ago, when humans changed into birds. That is how birds came to be. The birds hatched eggs, out of which came the first humans. Humans changed into trees but some changed into the wind; they were the ones who first blew breath from their mouths. From a gash in a mango tree came the sea, and the sea monsters who lived in it carved channels through the land. Humans also metamorphosed into yams, though only those who perform garden duties today know the secret of how they did it—just as only fishermen know how the sea monsters carved all those channels. Gardeners tell us they even know the names of the first humans who turned themselves into yams and who gave birth to yam children. Only they have this information, and they make much use of it in the incantation they utter at the annual ritual dedicated to yam growing, just as canoe makers and fishnet makers know exactly how the first canoes and fishnets metamorphosed.

In the time of creation, Nuakekepaki, a man who turned into a rock, lived underwater. He moved around under the open sea and wherever he saw a canoe he would overturn it. He needed the valuables in those canoes to pay the *kwesi,* or bride price, to his mother-in-law and her family. He still over-turns canoes today, though it has not been his duty since.

A woman of the first generation, named Anabuyueta, bore a son with many arms. She set him in fresh water where he curled up and nearly died. Then she placed him in the bitter sea water. This revived him, so he swam away and made his home in a rock cave on the sea floor. One day she went out to visit him, bringing with her some seed yams. To make them grow she charmed them. If we try to plant things in the sea today, they will die. But the seed of the yams grown in the sea by Anabuyueta is the seed the Green Parrot totem (clan) use today. And it is indeed no ordinary seed, for it descends from the garden of the Muruas Octopus.

The story of the swordfish brothers Tobwaliton and To-bebeso tells about the origin of the sea and these two super-natural monsters who constantly battled the rain-making forces that came with the summer monsoon: A huge mango tree once grew near Sawatupa. Under it slept a man, his wife, and their dog. When day broke, the man set off with his dog to gather food, leaving his wife in camp to cook and tend to the duties of the yam garden. Just as the man was about to depart, he noticed something wriggling beneath the bark of the tree. It looked like a fish, so he gave it to his wife to roast; but before she could grab hold of it, the dog bit off a piece and scampered into the bush. The man worried whether the fish might be poisonous, but at the end of the day the dog returned home unharmed by his dining experience. Same for his wife, who had consumed the rest of the fish: "Good food you gave me," she said. "Tomorrow early you go and cut down the mango tree."[3] Early next morning, they took their axes to the tree. All day they cut and cut but scarcely could they penetrate the tree's skin. The sun set and the exhausted couple went home. Next day they returned to continue chopping down the tree, but to their surprise its wound had healed—the tree's skin was completely closed. They returned a third day and a fourth with the same result. Finally, on the fifth day, they managed to hack out a slab of wood from the mango tree, so that during the night it could not completely close up because a part of it was missing. They burned the cut piece of wood to warm their hut.

Each day the couple continued cutting, always removing a piece until they finally felled the great mango tree. But suddenly water gushed forth out of its roots. It gushed and gushed and gushed until it submerged the tree, creating an entire ocean above it. The man, his wife, and his people now had nowhere to stand.

This is when Tobwaliton and Tobebeso appeared. As noses, they had long swords with short teeth. They passed swiftly over the sea and made it calm. Then they cut dirt out of the sea bottom to make the islands—Madalabuna Island, Nedaonara Island, Tewara, Sanaroa, Segata, Lesopi. Finally they came to the mountain island Solomanaki. At first the swordfish brothers meant to cut right through it, but instead they both lay on top of it. There they wriggled around to cut a lake into the mountain top and they filled it with fish. But some fish wanted to leave the ocean and live on dry land. They wanted to eat people but the people refused them access. As punishment, these fish made the sea bitter so that people can no longer drink it. Finally, the sister of Tobwaliton and Tobebeso took a seashell, charmed it, and stopped the water just short of reaching the island tops. They say the mango tree that caused it all still resides underneath the wide seas. Meanwhile the water continues to pour out of its roots. Some islanders claim they can see the root near Sawatupa, but they don't dare approach it in their canoes for fear it will open further and engulf what little remains of the level land where we Dobu plant our precious yams.

When the monsoon season changes from the southeast (winter) to the northwest (summer), the spirit ancestors are most active and the planting of yams begins. "This is when the palolo [worms] rule over the south-east monsoon; we take them from the reef, we cook and eat them; next morning, dead calm; then the north-west monsoon comes."[4]

This chant, uttered on the eve of the celebration of the worm's sighting by fishermen, expresses the excitement that accompanies delivery of the news (the shaking is likely a reference to earthquake tremors common in the region):

damasi budibudi	the deep sea palolo
kasa butu yoyoi	the village shakes from our running
butu yoyoinaia.	shakes from our running thither.
da geba doroebe	look there seawards
nabudibudiega	from their deep sea place
maina laulauolu	with yellow sunset glow
kasa butu yoyoi.	the village shakes from our running.[5]

17

How Our Islands Were Made

A SHINTO STORY

Crack open an egg and carefully empty the contents into a flat dish. Watch the dense bright yellow yolk rise, a perfectly round dome floating in the albumen, the translucent watery mass spreading out beneath. Now crack the shell of another egg and try separating it: first hold its contents in the larger half shell, then, touching the shell edges together, carefully empty as much of the slimy albumen as you can into the smaller half, holding back the yolk. Be careful not to rupture the yolk with the sharp shell edges. If you succeed, you will have achieved something like what the Shinto gods accomplished when they birthed the eight great islands of the archipelago of Japan. As in the scrambled-egg version of the Chinese Pan Gu myth, the archipelago started as a mass that was separated into lighter and darker matter, the densest forming dome-shaped parts around a center, with each dome and center rising above the vast ocean that surrounded it.

Japan is a watery, mountainous place comprising several

thousand islands dotted with active volcanoes and fault zones that give rise to violent earthquakes—nothing like the way it was before Kuniumi, the birth or formation of the country, when the primeval slush that comprised it lay in silence. At least two similar creation stories narrate the emergence myth. The one I have chosen to tell here is from William George Aston's translation of the *Nihongi*.[1]

Our story opens with the beginning of this creative process when the last pair of gods, the male Izanagi and female Izanami, consummate by mutual consent. As in the Polynesian myth, these parents from the union of masculine and feminine principles give birth to an abundance of children. The offspring are recognizable to anyone familiar with the Japanese landscape—they are powers of nature, particular islands, rivers, mountains, and trees, as well as the sun goddess and the moon god. In a nod to the trials of birthing and parenting, the fertile pair also create the unsatisfactory island of Ahaji (Awaji)—a volatile place. Located in a narrow strait connected to the inland Seto Sea, Ahaji is surrounded by powerful tidal whirlpools that create fast-moving currents, which result in sea levels that vary by as much as 1.5 meters (5 ft.). Running through Ahaji is the highly active Nojima fault zone, responsible for the 1995 Kobe earthquake that killed more than six thousand people.

Izanagi and Izanami also bear the fire god, who burns his mother to death as she delivers him. Perhaps feeling responsible, the male deity, Izanagi, follows Izanami into the Land of Yomi (the dead), where he views her rotting body as she is about to inhale her last breath. Embarrassed, she chases him away, but, having consumed the food of the underworld, she is no longer able to pass through the Aha gates in the narrow strait that separates the two worlds. As he flees toward eternal self-banishment on gloomy Ahaji, he "blows forth" and "blows out" several more creations. Could they be the eighteen major volcanoes that dot the archipelago alongside eroded mountains?

In the beginning the universe was silent and shapeless. At first the clearer, purer part was drawn out, like the white of an egg, while the heavier, more corporeal part was condensed toward the center. The finer element was lighter and easier to unite, so it rose to the top, and heaven formed first. Below that appeared Takamagahara (plain of high heaven) and the first clouds of heaven. Finally, the rest of the mass sank down and became the earth. The soil that would become the land at first floated around, the way a fish might play on the surface of the water.

Once heaven and earth were separated, a reed-shoot grew out of the water and was spontaneously transformed into three male deities: Kuni-toko-tachi no Mikoto, Kuni-no sa-tsuchi no Mikoto, and Toyo-kumu-nu no Mikoto. In the next generation more deities came forth: Uhiji-ni no Mikoto (Mud Earth), Suhiji-ni no Mikoto (Sand Earth), and still others. Finally, Iza-nagi no Mikoto (Male-who-invites) and Izanami no Mikoto (Female-who-invites) came into being. They were given their sex by the mutual action of heavenly and earthly principles.

One day Izanagi and Izanami were standing on the Floating Bridge of heaven, looking over the side and wondering—can there be a country down there? Together they took hold of the long jewel-spear of heaven and poked around below. They felt the tip of the spear touch the ocean. When they submerged it and pulled it up, the brine and silt dripping from it coagulated and became an island. They named it Ono-goro-jima (Spontaneously congealed island). The two descended and, finding it pleasant, decided to live on the little island. They also decided to marry. Izanami said, "In my body there is a place which is the source of femininity." Izanagi replied, "In my body

The Divine Couple looking down from the Bridge of
Heaven and wondering, "Can there be a country down there?"
(Kobayashi Eitaku, *Izanami and Izanagi Creating the Japanese
Islands,* mid-1880s, William Sturgis Bigelow Collection,
photograph copyright © Museum of Fine Arts, Boston)

there is a place which is the source of masculinity." Then he said, "I wish to unite this source-place of my body to the source-place of thy body."[2] She consented, and with that proposal the two became the first beings to unite as husband and wife. Their next step would be to produce island children. They began by making Ono-goro-jima, a great pillar at the center of the island.

When it was time to give birth to their firstborn child, the island of Ahaji was to be the placenta; but the parents weren't very content with it. They called it Ahaji-no-Shima (Unsatisfactory Island). Next they produced Oho-yamato no Toyo-aki-tsushima (Rich Harvest Island). Then they produced Iyo no futa-na and Tsukushi, then twin islands Oki and Sado, followed by Koshi, Oho-shima, and Kibi no ko—eight births in all. Two more islands, Tsushima and Iki, and other small islands were contrived out of coagulated saltwater foam. They called their newly created land Oho-ya-shima, the Great Eight Island Country.

Once this was done Izanami and Izanagi gave birth to the sea, then the rivers, then the mountains, and the Ku-ku-no-chi, the ancestor of trees and Kaya no hime, the ancestor of herbs. To rule over their islands, the husband and wife decided to produce a being. They made the Sun-Goddess, Oho-hiru-me no muchi. As a child the Sun-Goddess was very lustrous; walking the landscape, she beautifully illuminated all six quarters of the island world: North, East, South, West, Above, and Below. She quickly became her parents' favorite, for they knew she was destined for greater things. "We have had many children," they said, "but none of them have been equal to this wondrous infant. She ought not to be kept long in this land, but we ought of our own accord to send her at once to Heaven, and entrust to her the affairs of Heaven."[3] Since heaven and earth were not yet so distantly separated, they sent her up by the ladder they had fabricated to make their descent.

Next Izanami and Izanagi gave birth to the Moon-God. He was not quite as brilliant as his older sister. Still they chose him to share in her responsibility, so they sent him to heaven as well. But then the good fortune in parenting of Izanami and Izanagi began to go awry. It began when they bore the Leech-Child. Even when he was three years old he was unable to stand upright, so they laid him in the rock-camphor-wood boat of heaven and abandoned it to the winds. Next came Sosa no wo no Mikoto, the Impetuous One. He was fierce tempered—always throwing crying tantrums and performing cruel acts. His tears are the reason why the green mountains of the Great Eight Island Country have become so badly eroded. After all their other efforts to calm Sosa failed, his parents confronted him directly. Because he was so wicked he was unfit to rule over any part of this world. So they expelled him to the netherworld. Next born came the even more evil Fire God, Kagu tsuchi. He set fire to his own mother Izanami, but not before she delivered Hani-yama-hime, the Earth-Goddess, and Midzu-ha-no-me, the Water-Goddess. Then the Fire God took the Earth-Goddess as his wife. They bore Waka-musubi (Young Growth), whose crown on her head produced the silkworm and the mulberry tree and whose navel bore the five kinds of grain.

Greatly disturbed, Izanagi pursued wounded Izanami into the Land of Yomi—the world of the dead. She begged her husband not to look upon her in her awful condition, but Izanagi couldn't resist one last glance at his loved one before she passed. He lit a torch to illuminate her, but when he witnessed the putrefying matter gushing out of her body, he became horrified, fleeing at the sight of the hideous and polluted land they together had created. Because she had already consumed the food of Yomi and was no longer permitted to reenter the world of the living, Izanami sent a cadre of females to pursue and taint her husband for deserting her.

On the way back, Izanagi raced between the narrow gate of Haya-sufu-na (Quick Such Name), where the ocean tide is very strong. After he purified himself in the sea waters, he blew out—he erupted—creating Iha-tsu-tsu no Mikoto (Rock of Elder), Oho-nawo-bi no Kami (Great Pattern of Person), and Sokotsutsu no Mikoto (Bottom Elder). On the next tide he produced Oho-aya-tsu-bi no Kami (Great Remedy Person), and on the next Aka-tsutsu no Mikoto (Red Elder), then on succeeding tides many other deities of heaven and earth, as well as the Sea-Plain. Finally, exhausted and disappointed by so many of his unintended adverse acts and creations, Izanagi returned to the place that was his first child—the unsatisfactory island of Ahaji. There he built himself an abode of gloom and lived forever in silence and concealment.

18

Haudenosaunee Island Making

The Haudenosaunee (People of the longhouse), popularly known as the Iroquois, live in the northeast United States, south and east of the Great Lakes.[1] Before the advent of the European intruders they comprised a confederacy consisting of the Cayuga, Onondaga, Mohawk, Seneca, Oneida, and, later, Tuscarora tribes. Because the native peoples of the eastern United States have been influenced by Christianity since early colonial times, Old and New Testament elements have deeply penetrated their stories of creation. Nonetheless, indigenous natural elements, such as the watery environment and the power of the west wind, are recognizable to anyone familiar with this region, especially during winter, when "lake effect" snow, driven by the west wind, piles up.

I decided to place the Earth Diver myth here, among other island-based creation stories, because the Haudenosaunee conceive of the world as having grown from an island. This is not surprising if you look at a map of their habitat, which is surrounded by water—the Great Lakes on the north and west, the Saint Lawrence Seaway flowing to the North Atlantic on the northeast, and the glacially formed Finger Lakes to the south.[2]

A very long time ago there was no land, only water and the creatures who swam in it—turtles and fish, otters and musk-rats. The Air World above the clouds was where the water birds soared. Above all of that lay Sky World (Karonhia:ke), a place inhabited by humans who look like us but had much more power: they could make things happen just by thinking. These Sky People lived happy lives; they never died, nor was anyone ever born—until Sky Woman, wife of the Sky World Chief, became pregnant and asked for a drink of tea made from the roots of the Tree of Life, a giant tree that grew in the center of the Sky World, on which grew many kinds of fruit and whose flowers lit up the skyscape. When the chief dug at the roots, the dirt caved in. This left a huge hole in Sky World; and when, out of curiosity, Sky Woman leaned over to take a peek through the hole, she lost her balance and fell through the opening. (Others say she knew from a dream that she was destined to do so and jumped.) As she descended, she reached out to grab hold of a branch from the fallen tree, tore out a handful of seeds, and plummeted to the watery world below.

A flock of birds—some say they were geese, others swans, still others herons—happened to be flying through Air World. They made a large blanket out of their wings and managed to catch Sky Woman.

They safely lowered her. But to where? Sky Woman couldn't live in Water World because she was unable to swim. Suddenly a giant turtle came to the rescue. He told the birds to place their burden on his back. And there they gently settled her. Sky Woman thanked the animals, but she became con-cerned that there was barely enough space to move around on the back of the turtle. She needed solid ground to live on.

Haudenosaunee Sky Woman lands on earth, thanks to a
flock of birds. (Illustration by John Kahionhes Fadden)

Eager to help, one by one the water creatures dove down deep
to try to get dirt from under the water. Toads, frogs, otters—
they all failed. Finally, some say, it was the tiny muskrat who
succeeded in bringing a few grains of mud-covered sand up
from below. Sky Woman placed the dirt on the back of the turtle. She sang and danced in a counter-clockwise direction—the
way you see the stars move across the sky when you look toward the north country. With that the turtle's shell grew and
the grains of dirt multiplied. Its surface grew so large that it
became the entire continent of North America. Today we call
our country Turtle Island. Then Sky Woman took the seeds
she had held tightly in her hand and cast them over the land.
They grew right away into grass and trees and bushes—all the
plants that populate the world as far as we can see.

 In time Sky Woman gave birth to a baby girl, Tekawerahkwa, who grew up with her mother's valuable knowledge

and insight of the worlds above and below. Her mother told her not to venture to the west, where danger lingered. But out of curiosity, her young daughter failed to heed her mother's warning. There she was confronted by a strong wind and a dark cloud harboring the outline of a male being. He is the powerful wind that brings winter storms across the big lakes. Tekawerahkwa fainted, and when she woke up she discovered she had become the bride of the Spirit of the West Wind, who had fallen in love with her. Out of their union Tekawerahkwa bore twin sons, Teharonghyawago, or Sapling, who was kind and gentle, and Tawiskaron, or Flint, who was cold-hearted and troublesome. Sadly, Tekawerahkwa died in childbirth because Flint pushed his way out of her armpit trying to be born first; but Sapling, who created all good things, took care to place the head of his mother in the sky, where she would become the moon. Thus she would forever have power over the waters—the tides—and night timekeeping. Out of the remnants of Tekawerahkwa's body the three sisters—corn, beans, and squash—would grow to make up our sustenance. From her heart grew sacred tobacco used to communicate with the Creator, and her feet became the wild strawberry, the Great Medicine.

Under the watchful eyes of their father and grandmother, the twins grew up. They were given the task of creating everything else found in the world surrounding us today. Sapling created all the beauty on earth—the rivers and mountains. He taught the birds to sing and the water creatures to dance. He made the rainbows and the gentle rain. Flint issued creations of his own—but they were bad. He added dangerous rapids to his brother's rivers, and out of wind and water he made hurricanes. Alongside the medicinal plants that Sapling created, Flint planted poisonous berries and roots. Sapling made useful animals and plants that people could easily eat, while Flint put thorns on the berry bushes and bones in the fish. Sapling made the doves, the mockingbird, and the partridge, while Flint created wolves, bears, snakes—and giant mosquitoes. The brothers also made human beings good and bad. The good ones made by Sapling learned to take only what they needed for nourishment and leave the rest for others, but Flint's bad ones neglected their duties and became wasteful.[3]

Still, Turtle Island was kept more or less in balance. Then one day Flint decided to steal all the animals—even the timid deer and stately elk; he imprisoned them in a huge cave. Sapling followed him there and when Flint wasn't tending the cave he broke the gate, sneaked inside, and set all the animals free. Seeking revenge, Flint confronted Sapling and put it to him directly: "Brother, what do you think there is on earth, with which you might be killed?" Answered Sapling: Only "the foam of the billows of the [Great] Lake." Then he posed the same question to his evil brother: "What do you think would take your life?" "Nothing except horn or flint," snapped Flint.[4] This set the stage for a future encounter that would change this world.

Seeking the most effective plan to do away with his evil brother, Sapling befriended a young male deer that shed its antlers during autumn each year. He noticed that their replacements got bigger and bigger with each shedding. Finally, after seven years the deer, now grown up to be a stately buck, offered his giant antlers to aid the good brother in his conquest. When the brothers finally confronted one another, Flint hurled froth and foam from the Great Lake at Sapling—all to no avail. Then Sapling went on the attack, giant antler in hand, and, after a long struggle, won the battle. Since neither brother—unlike us ordinary humans—could ever die, Flint limped off in disgrace, but not before uttering these last words: "I have gone to the far west. All the races of men will follow me . . . when they die."[5]

19

Diving in the Mud

A CHEROKEE CREATION STORY

This story originated in the Appalachian mountains of western North Carolina, part of the U.S. territory inhabited by the Cherokee (which also included most of the states of North and South Carolina, Georgia, Alabama, and Tennessee) until 1838, when they were forced by the government to move far from their original homeland, to Oklahoma. Before their first European encounter with De Soto in 1540, the Cherokee were an advanced agricultural society, producing corn, beans, squash, pumpkins, and sunflowers, along with many other crops. Though the story tells how their mountains were made, it also incorporates the Haudenosaunee idea of their home as an island, which is mainly why I have chosen to place it here. Because the Haudenosaunee and the Cherokee belong to a common language group, it is no surprise that aspects of their origin myths are shared. Like the Amazonian story "Salt of the Earth," which migrated down from the high Andes, this tale exemplifies mythic substitution in an alternate environment. Social issues that concern us today are part of the story as well: Will the world of the future be as plagued with unbridled reproduction as the one they descended from?[1]

In the beginning all was water. All the animals lived above the sky vault, which was made of solid rock. They lived in a land called Galun'lati (Galunlati), which means "Gift of God." Galun'lati is also the dwelling place of mythical creatures, such as the horned serpent, Uktena, and the home of nature's most exaggerated things. There mountains are taller, forests are denser, and storms are more violent. It was very crowded—and the animals needed more room. As they looked down at the water, they wondered what lay below. One day Dayuni'si, the Water Beetle, so named because he was able to walk on water, volunteered to go down and check things out. He descended and prowled about, but he couldn't find a solid piece of land where he could rest. So he dove down into the deep water and came up with some soft mud. It started to grow and spread out on all sides until it became an island. This island gradually grew into what we now call earth. Floating on the water, the island was fastened to the sky vault with four cords, one at each corner.

At first our Cherokee land was flat and mushy. When the birds, anxious to get down, tried to alight on it, they found little support and were forced to head back to crowded Galun'lati. They sent the Great Buzzard who flapped his wings downward; as the wings struck the soft ground, they made impressions that became valleys. When he raised his wings, the mud welled up into mountains. He got so carried away with his mountain making that the animals needed to call him back. That's why Cherokee country today is so mountainous.

As the earth dried out a bit more, the animals gradually ventured down from the sky. It was very dark, so they got hold of the sun and set it on a track to go across the earth every day from east to west. But it got too hot, so they raised the sun a handbreadth higher. Still it was too hot, so they raised it another handbreadth, and another . . . until it reached seven handbreadths. Each day the sun moves beneath the arch along the height of the seventh handbreadth and goes back west to east at night on the upper side.

Below there's another world just like ours, except the seasons are different. The streams that come down from the mountains are the trails that reach this underworld and the springs are the rivers' beginnings—the doorways where we can enter it. To get there, you need to fast and you must have an underworld guide. We know the seasons are reversed down there because the water in the springs is warmer in winter and cooler than the outer air in summer.

When the animals and plants were first made, they were told to watch and keep awake for seven nights. Most of them made it through the first night, but on the second several more dropped off—still more on the third and fourth—until by the seventh night, only the owl, the panther, and one or two more animals were still keeping watch. These animals were given the power to see in the dark and make prey of the ones who slept at night. Of the trees only the cedar, the spruce, the holly, and the laurel stayed awake to the end. This is why they acquired the power to remain always green and to be the best medicine. The other trees were told they needed to lose their hair each winter.

Last of all came the people, at first only a brother and a sister—until he struck her with a fish. Seven days later she gave birth to a child, and seven days after to another, and another. . . . The people increased in number so fast that, like Galun'lati, the earth was in danger of not being able to hold them all. So it was decided that a woman should have only one child a year.[2]

Some day when the earth grows old and worn out and all the plants, animals, and people die, the cords that hold up the world will break; then the earth will sink down and all will return to water again. We are afraid of this.

PART FIVE

EXTREMES

Ultima Thule is a nickname given by astronomers to Kuiper Belt Object 2014MU69, one of the most remote objects in the solar system. The name is appropriate: Thule (Qaanaaq), Greenland, is one of the northernmost towns in the world, and in ancient times, its inhabitants, both the Norse (Viking) and the indigenous Inuit, imagined a dangerous world to the north, beyond the borders of the known world. Norse invaders spoke of the forthcoming day when they would experience Fimbulwinter—a winter like none before in the midst of a time of extreme climate change. That would be followed by Ragnarök—the cataclysmic end of the world. So goes the climax of the rather gloomy Norse story of creation, which opens with the emergence of a race of giant warlike gods out of the hissing, melting borderland where ice on the north meets fire on the south.

The Inuit creation story—one of many from the far northern indigenous inhabitants of Alaska and northern Canada as well as Greenland—features a race of primeval beings who, like the seasonal landscape, are capable of self-transformation. Their first children emerged from holes in the snow. So did walruses, seals, and their dogs (to help them hunt bears). In their spare time the gods in heaven still amuse themselves by playing a game of football—a spectacle we see as the northern lights.

On the opposite side of the globe, along the southern tip of South America, an extinct culture once called the Haush witnessed the violent clash of two vast oceans. The creation story they passed on tells of battles that still rage between sea, wind, and cannibal monsters who entice to their death any who would dare navigate the strait that separates the mainland from the "beyond world"—the uninhabited island at land's end.

20

Norse Creation

MURDER ON ICE

People who live in the land of the midnight sun experience two climates. Summer is green, warm, and nurturing, while winter is cold and stormy, with skies torn apart by lightning and thunder and the surrounding craggy mountains blanketed in snow.[1] The Norse creation myth tells of a multitude of giant deities who personify the natural forces that threaten the lives of Scandinavian and northern Germanic people. The first of these is Ymir, who emerges from a melting mass of ice and represents the chaos that existed prior to creation. His story culminates in the rise of Odin, a later-generation hero deity who dismembers Ymir's body and uses the parts to create culture. Forming the world out of the body parts of a defeated enemy is a theme we have encountered before, for example in the Babylonian, Chinese, Mande, and Haudenosaunee myths. The Norse story ends in Ragnarök, a series of apocalyptic battles accompanied by natural disasters and the submersion of the landscape. But will a rebirth happen?

Those who live there say that once there were two lands that
bordered on one another: Muspelheim, the world of ice to the
north, and Niflheim, the world of fire to the south. Between
the two lay Ginnungagap—a dark, violent abyss where the
frost from one side collided with flames from the other. At the
point of contact, like droplets of water coming in contact with
a hot stove, they hissed, sizzled, and let off huge clouds of
steam—fire and ice engaging in an eternal battle, each bent on
destroying the other. The droplets eventually condensed and
magically came alive in the form of a god-like giant. He called
himself Ymir, the Screamer, and he possessed destructive powers. While he slept, an entire race of evil giants—the Vanir—
had exited from his armpits and leg joints. As the frost continued to melt, a cow emerged. She nurtured Ymir with her milk.
One day, as she was licking the frost to acquire its nurturing
salts, Ymir noticed the shape of a head beginning to emerge
from the icy rocks. On the second day its hair was visible, and
by the third day the full figure of a tall, powerful, and hand-
some man came out of the dissolved mass. His heart was warm,
and he was good. This giant called himself Buri, the Progenitor, the first of the Aesir tribe of gods. His grandson, named
Odin, would become the greatest chief of all the Aesir god
clans. He and his two brothers were destined to be the sworn
enemies of Ymir and his race of giants.

  After many years of good and evil living together precar-
iously in the world, Odin and his brothers decided that they
must—once and for all—destroy Ymir and his kind. They at-
tacked Ymir, and after a hard-fought battle they killed him.
When huge Ymir toppled over, a vast river of blood flowed
from his wounds. It flooded his domain and drowned all of his
kin, except for a grandchild, Bergelmir, who survived with his
wife by hiding in a chest, thus becoming the progenitor of the
Vanir clan of deities.

Odin and his brothers create the world out of
the body of Ymir. (Lorenz Frølich, *Odin, Vili,
and Vé Create the World Out of Ymir's Body*)

At this time things were not as we know them in the real
world. It was left to the victors to create the world out of the
remains of their slain enemy. So Odin and his brothers dragged
Ymir's corpse down to the bottom of the icy realm. From it
they created the earth, the sea on top of it, and the heavens at
the very top. Ymir's blood became the ocean, rivers and lakes,
and springs; his long bones the mountains; his teeth and broken bones the sand pebbles. They made day and night too. Day

was fair and bright—more like the warm-hearted Aesir race—
but night was dark and gloomy, bearing more traits that re-
sembled those of the Vanir clan. To light the world the Aesir
gods caught sparks and cinders blown in from the southern
world of fire. Thus they created the sun, moon, and stars, setting each in motion in its own time cycle. They called the sun
Sol and the moon Mani. Odin gave each of them a chariot and
a pair of swift horses to propel them across the sky. From Ymir's
round skull Odin made the dome of the sky. Ymir's brains became the billowy clouds, his hair the trees, plants, grass, and
flowers. His skin and muscles were turned into the soil. They
wasted no part of Ymir's body. The Aesir gods even used his
eyebrows to build a high fence around the world to protect the
race of people they planned to create to inhabit their beautiful
new world.

But first the gods needed to create their own city, Asgard,
a place beyond the ocean, in a country much colder than the
green country (Midgard) they had prepared for their real people. The city would be in heaven where the Aesir could look
down on their people and protect them from any surviving
evil giants from Ymir's clan. The two worlds would be connected by a bridge of many colors—the rainbow we recognize
today.

Now that Odin and his brothers had set the stage, they
were ready to commence their most important creation—
people. To make the first living beings, Odin and his brothers
took the maggots from the decaying body of Ymir and created
a race of dwarfs. These first people were wise and skilled, but
they behaved more like Ymir than Odin. Four of the dwarfs
were assigned the task of holding up Ymir's sky skull—each
stationed in one of the cardinal directions: north, east, south,
and west. They also created a race of taller people who lived
on the surface and behaved more like the Aesir. Preferring the

cold darkness, the dwarfs migrated to caves deep in the ground, where they spent their days digging precious jewels and metals embedded in the rocks. They took them to their foundry where they heated and hammered them, crafting beautiful ornaments out of the earth's abundant valuable resources. Unfortunately, the subterranean dwarfs and the surface dwellers became mutual enemies. The dwarfs say it was because the tall people continually lusted after their gold and jewels.

The gods were dissatisfied with their handiwork. They truly wished to make manifest their love and protection. So they crossed the rainbow bridge and came down to earth. As they walked along the seashore they selected a pair of trees: an ash and an elm. Odin breathed on them and they turned into a living man and woman. One brother touched their heads and they became wise. The other brother touched their faces, enabling them to speak, hear, and see. Ask, the Ash, and Embla, the Elm, became the father and mother of a new race destined to dwell in Midgard under the watchful eyes of their Aesir creators.

The Norse say that someday Ragnarök, the Apocalypse, the fate of men and gods, will come. It will begin with a great winter such as no one has ever seen.[2] The winds will blow unceasingly and snow will descend from all directions. The sun, moon, and stars will disappear from the sky, leaving the earth in darkness. People will starve and lose all sense of their goodness. Even among their own family they will fight for survival. Loki, a traitor to the Aesir gods, will sail his ship carrying an army of giants over the flooded earth, destroying everything in its path. Wolves will come out of the hills and eat the weakest of their human prey.

Then Fenrir, the monster-wolf who resides in the swamps, will race over the land eating everything in its path. His lower jaw will touch the ground and his upper jaw the top of the sky—he won't miss anything. Jormungand, the ocean serpent, will spit his venom over land and water, poisoning everything in his wake. Then the sky will split open and fire serpents brighter than the sun will emerge through its cracks. They will cross the rainbow bridge, destroying every fragment of it as they pass. Odin will be forced to summon his good gods, who have been kept safely in Asgard, to battle. But they already will know the outcome of Ragnarök and, though they will fight valiantly, they will be destined to lose the war against the forces of destruction. Fenrir will swallow Odin and his men.

In the end Vidar, son of Odin, will avenge his father's death. He will charge Fenrir and, holding its mouth open, plunge his sword down the giant wolf's throat, slaying him. Even Thor, god of thunder and lightning, the mightiest of all the Norse gods and defender of the Aesir from the encroachment of giants, will meet his fate. Though Thor will slay the serpent Jormungand with his hammer, he will end up so full of the venom that he will be able to recede only a few steps from the battleground before toppling over dead. In this series of one-on-one Ragnarök contests all the gods will do themselves in, as the world sinks slowly into the dark sea. The creation undone, all will become as it was in the beginning—a void looking as if nothing had ever happened. But others say a rebirth will occur. Creation will happen all over again, when a new green and beautiful earth rises out of the ocean.[3]

21

Arctic Inuit Creation

The land along the Arctic Ocean is as inhospitable a place to live as any on the planet. Long dark winters, with frigid temperatures, raging snowstorms, and shifting winds, followed by treacherous melting ice in the summer, mean that finding food and the other basic necessities of life is a dangerous struggle. Yet a hardy ethnic group of 150,000 people survive on the 5,000 kilometer (3,000 mi.) stretch of land that runs from Alaska across Canada to Greenland. They call themselves the Inuit (Real People), and, given the threatening circumstances under which most of them live, it is not surprising that stories of where they came from and how they got there are filled with the fears that preoccupy them. Like Norseland, the land- and skyscape of the Inuit are highly transformative, with seasonal extremes of green and white, light and dark. The people and animals who appear in these stories mirror the places they inhabit—all are capable of self-transformation.[1]

How did it all come to exist? Once long ago the whole earth— the soil, hills, stones, snow, and ice—just dropped down from above. At first it was impossible to stand up because the sky was so close to the ground—until the first humans and animals who originally lived huddled together below decided to set up pillars, one in each of the four directions, to prop up the sky. But the pillars were not strong enough. They became dislocated, causing the world to tilt. Then a pouring rain came down and drowned everything. The islands in the sea where everyone sought refuge tipped over. You can still see the remains of the original creatures' shells and bones on the island tops today.

We think there must have been another living world underneath us, also supported by four pillars. That's because of the driftwood we pick up along the shore—it must be all that's left of the underground forest, the world where we Inuit came from. First, two Inuit men emerged from out of the ground. They were made out of *niaquqtaak* (mounds of earth). They ate of the earth. These two Inuit wanted to reproduce, so one took the other to be his wife-man. The wife-man became pregnant, but when the time came there was no way for the child to get born. So the husband sang a magical song to the pregnant wife-man.[2] The singing made the penis split and the wife-man was transformed into a woman. Most of us Inuit descend from the two of them.

Unfortunately, not all women could get pregnant. They needed to go out in search of children of the earth. Babies came out of the earth, covered with leaves from the snowbanks among the willow bushes. There they lay sprawled out with their eyes closed. They couldn't even crawl. The women went out in the snow and found the babies. They adopted them and brought them home. They made clothes for them and nurtured them. Soon there were many Inuit populating the world. They needed to get food to eat and fur to protect their bodies, but it was too dark to hunt. All they could get were ptarmigan and hare who lived nearby. They would shoot them with the bow and arrow.

Ravens wanted light, too, so they could better find their food, but foxes preferred the dark—the better to pillage the caches where the Inuit people hid their meat. The two got into a big argument. "Qau! Qau! May the light come, may the day come!," said the raven.³ "Taaq! Taaq! May it be night, may it be night!," the fox responded.⁴ With these magical spoken words they settled the argument by alternating between the two. And it has been that way ever since.

Now we Inuit realized we needed the help of the animals to hunt. We needed dogs. So a man went out with harnesses in hand and began to stamp on the ground and call out. Suddenly dogs sprang out of tiny little earthen mounds that peaked above the snow. They shook themselves off. From then on men with their team of dogs could track big game—bear and walrus and seal—from much farther away and bring it back home.

Before day and night, there was no death. People just grew older and older and when they could no longer walk or see, they would just lie down. With death also came the sun, moon, and stars. So now when people die they can go up to heaven and become luminous.

Once the heavens were created and death solved the problem of an overcrowded world, the spirits of the departed ones needed to amuse themselves. In heaven they played a game of football using the head of a walrus for the ball. On certain nights you can hear the swishing sound as the empty skull turns around in flight and the "chunk" sound when the walrus tusks stick in the ground. And you can actually see the *aqsarniit* (players), shimmering draperies of light, some like rays, others crooked and waving in changing shapes as they move swiftly in all directions. Some are bright pink in color, others red, some green and yellow. They meet all together overhead, as if in a huddle, then they fly off in all directions. As one of our young girls tells it:

> When we were children ... I used to see different coloured *aqsarniit*—some were bright pink in colour. I had heard it said that the *aqsarniit* cut peoples' heads off. I tended to believe this because I was also aware of the saying that the *aqsarniit* used walrus heads for footballs, and so I was scared of them! I think it has something to do with the speed they go at: if they touch your head then it will be cut off. Although I never heard of anyone losing their head because of the *aqsarniit,* they still feel frightening. The other thing was that when we whistled at them they would make swishing sounds and would pick up speed. Seeing this made me really terrified thinking that they would indeed cut off my head. Of course that was a child's way of thinking about them.[5]

Uangnaq (the northwest wind) is the strongest of all our winds. She comes down in the winter during the short daytime. She blows in constantly, creating huge crescent-shaped drifts with cusps pointing to the direction from which she came. No sooner has she accomplished this than she destroys her creation by blowing away the tips of the drifts and forming each into round tongue shapes—then a third shape with ridges and a sharp point.

Fortunately, she comes down at night. In the summer Nigiq comes down. He blows from the southeast, but not as strong as Uangnaq; however, he does blow constantly. The drifts he makes are all pretty much the same, with smooth little ridges and tapered, but they don't change much:

> *Nigiq* has a man *inua* while *Uangnaq* has a woman *inua*. When the woman with her words intimidates him, he does not get agitated as a woman would under the circumstances. He is able to cope with this intimidation for a length of time. That is why he is able to smooth things over, whereas, as always, a woman will make things rough.

That, of course, is one man's interpretation. Here's another:

> In the past . . . women settled down for the night by removing their footwear [ready to retire]. As for the southeast wind, in the manner that men are active in the middle of the night going from household to household, so too will this wind become active and stronger during the night.[6]

Winds are a lot like people.

Thunder and lightning were created in bygone days. Once two orphaned children got left behind when their people were transferring campsites, moving their goods across a great river. At a loss for food and carrying only the clothes on their backs, they decided to head back and sort through any remains that might help them sustain themselves. The girl found a firestone, and her brother came across a stiff, dried-out piece of caribou skin. Thinking about what to do with these things, the boy said: "Sister, we will be human beings no longer; but what shall we be?" "Caribou," suggested his sister. "No, for then we would be gored to death," answered her brother. "Sister, what shall we be?" "Seals," his sister suggested. "No, for then we would be torn to death."[7]

They went on naming all the animals they could think of to change into, but each time they realized how they could be harmed. Finally the little girl suggested lightning and thunder. So they became just that by turning themselves into spirits of the air and rushing across the sky, the sister striking sparks with the firestone while the brother pounded his piece of dry caribou skin like a drum. The heavens roared as the children rose up into the sky.

Later the two orphans avenged themselves for being left behind by making thunder and lightning over the new campsite. When travelers later entered the desolate place they found all the people lying dead in and outside their tents. They had no wounds—only a redness in their eyes from terror. But when the travelers touched them they crumbled to ashes. This is how people discovered the dangers of thunder and lightning. Since then when thunder is heard from the striking of the skin drum and the sparks seen from the firestone of the lightning, the spirits come alive. And people shoot an arrow in the direction whence they came.[8]

22

Tierra Del Fuego

WHERE THE SEAS CLASH

There are few areas on earth that were once occupied by human beings but are uninhabited today. The eastern end of Tierra del Fuego, at the tip of South America, is one of these. Isla de los Estados (Staten Island, from the Dutch), also called Jáius, is the place where the Atlantic and Pacific collide, and to this day, except for a small naval station, it remains unsettled. Jáius is separated from the large horn-shaped island of Tierra del Fuego by Le Maire Strait, long known for its extreme tides and dangerous currents. The wind blows perpetually from the west, bringing with it frequent storms and precipitation more than 250 days of the year.

Nomadic hunters known as the Haush lived on the western side of the strait until the nineteenth century. Before they were killed off by disease introduced by European intruders or absorbed by the Selk'nam people who lived farther to the west, they hunted whales and subsisted on guanaco (a llama-like mammal) in one of the most brutal places on earth. When Darwin left the area following his voyage on HMS *Beagle*, he described the place as desolate, with swells from the open ocean raging incessantly on scattered rock. He wrote in his diary: "One sight of such a coast is enough to make a landsman dream for a week about shipwrecks, peril, and death; and with this sight we bade farewell forever to Tierra del Fuego."[1]

The fathers and mothers of the world say that their ancestors never visited the island of Jáius, for they had no canoes. But all of us can see it looking east across the strait on a clear day. That place was the great cordillera of the east—one of the four that hold up the sky—and the seat of the major power of the universe.

Shenu (Wind), the powerful magician of the west, once fought a great battle in the strait with Kox (Sea), the magician of the north. Their fighting produced a huge storm. Wind emerged victorious in that battle, but, not pleased with the result, Sea brought forth a pair of Chénums (female cannibal monsters), one from the north, the other from the west, to engage in another fight in the middle of the strait. The monster of the north grabbed hold of her natural enemy from the west and tore her open. Her blood spurted from the middle of the strait all the way inland to where the River Irigoyen enters the sea. This is why the water flowing out of the peat bogs there has a reddish color. The Chénums once controlled all the rivers until Wind transformed them into the stone cliffs and precipices along the coasts.

These Chénums are still perched there on the high bluffs along the coast. You can see them lying in wait for their victims. They once enticed the people of the primeval world and when their victims came in for a closer look, they were swept helplessly up onto the beach. There the cannibals devoured them. The north cannibal remains alive in the strait's waters, where she incites violent combat in the seas. It is still a danger to seamen who dare pass through the strait instead of sailing around Cape Horn via the east end of Jáius. The wrecks of many ships remind us of the battles engaged there between Sea and Wind.

Now the wife of Sea and sister of Wind gave birth to many daughters—the whales. Their father created the great oceans to keep them from being eaten by powerful enemies. He carried them there in his arms to keep them safe. Others say the strait was once a lagoon and the sea opened it up to offer his daughters a safe passage from the pursuing evil forces. The jagged mountains of Jáius visible across the strait are the ramparts of a great fortress that separates us from the "be-yond world" of Pémaukel (East Sky), also called K'oin-Harri, or Cordillera-Root. This is all we know.

One day around the beginning of spring, a man came out of his hut and saw an ibis flying overhead. He became excited and shouted out to his family, "Look! An ibis is flying over our hut! Spring has arrived, the ibises are coming back." Everyone leapt for joy. But when the ibis heard these pretentious cries regarding his appearance, he became angry and caused a snow-storm. It snowed without stopping and became icy cold. The land and sea became completely covered with ice—they were frozen. It got so cold that people couldn't go out in search of food. They couldn't even find firewood because everything was hidden under a blanket of snow. Many of them died.

After a long time the snow ceased and the sun came out. Its heat got so intense that it melted all the ice and snow. Vast volumes of water started to flow in narrow and wide channels so that now the people could use their canoes to go out in search of food. But high on the hillsides and in some of the valleys the ice was too deep and the heat could not melt it. These are the glaciers that reach all the way to the sea—reminders of the great snowstorm caused by the ibis. Since then we have treated the ibis with great respect. We think of it as a sensitive and delicate woman who appreciates being held in high esteem. Now when ibises come close to camp, we remain still and silent and instruct our children not even to look at them.[2]

EPILOGUE

From the Ancient Greeks to the Big Bang

Though it was written down long ago, in the first century BCE, the narrative here will sound astonishingly familiar to many readers. Cast in unmistakably scientific-sounding language, it sounds almost *too* contemporary—too precise and rational to be thought of as a myth. In fact, some historians of science regard this story as a hallmark of the foundation of contemporary scientific method.[1] The Greek historian Diodorus Siculus (Diodorus of Sicily), the author of this creation story, drew inspiration from the Greek natural philosophers of Miletus on the coast of Asia Minor who lived five hundred years before he did and formulated their original—now largely lost—story line from careful observations of the landscape around them.[2] Diodorus's monumental universal history, *Biblioteca Historica*, covers everything from the creation of the world through the Trojan War and the exploits of Alexander the Great to the period of his own life. The early part of this work leaves no doubt in my mind that his version is indeed a source of the modern scientific take on cosmogenesis. It begins by addressing the question: How did the world begin?

When in the beginning . . . the universe was being
formed, both heaven and earth were indistinguish-
able in appearance, since their elements were inter-
mingled: then, when their bodies separated from
one another, the universe took on in all its parts
the ordered form in which it is now seen; the air set
up a continual motion, and the fiery element in it
gathered into the highest regions, since anything of
such a nature moves upward by reason of its lightness (and it is for this reason that the sun and the
multitude of other stars became involved in the universal whirl); while all that was mud-like and thick
and contained an admixture of moisture sank because of its weight into one place; and as this continually turned about upon itself and became com-
pressed, out of the wet it formed the sea, and out of
what was firmer, the land, which was like potter's
clay and entirely soft.[3]

Who could have dreamed up such a tale of indescribable
things chaotically mixed together that gradually sorted itself
out into a universe of land and water, sun and stars, now familiar to us? And where does the swollen, swampy land of changing degrees of firmness fit into the picture? Diodorus quickly
moves on to a second question: Where did we come from?

But as the sun's fire shone upon the land, it first of
all became firm, and then, since its surface was in a
ferment because of the warmth, portions of the wet
swelled up in masses in many places, and in these
pustules covered with delicate membranes made
their appearance. Such a phenomenon can be seen

even yet in swamps and marshy places whenever, the ground having become cold, the air suddenly and without any gradual change becomes intensely warm.

And while the wet was being impregnated with life by reason of the warmth in the manner described, by night the living things forthwith received their nourishment from the mist that fell from the enveloping air, and by day were made solid by the intense heat; and finally, when the embryos had attained their full development and the membranes had been thoroughly heated and broken open, there was produced every form of animal life. Of these, such as had partaken of the most warmth set off to the higher regions, having become winged, and such as retained an earthy consistency came to be numbered in the class of creeping things and of the other land animals, while those whose composition partook the most of the wet element gathered into the region congenial to them, receiving the name of water animals. And since the earth constantly grew more solid through the action of the sun's fire and of the winds, it was finally no longer able to generate any of the larger animals, but each kind of living creature was now begotten by breeding with one another.[4]

To judge by what Diodorus tells us, the original storytellers seem to have directed their highly perspicacious eyes toward their natural environment. They also seem to have been practical minded, for the story goes on to tell how humans were generated from living entities formed within fish-like creatures as embryos, which gradually reached maturity. Finally, we burst out—men and women—ready to learn how to fend for ourselves.

At first life was difficult. The earliest people lived like wild beasts, hunting and gathering on their own, continually under attack by predators—until they learned to come to one another's aid, Diodorus tells us. They also learned to communicate by articulating their simple vocal sounds into a language grounded in agreed-on symbols. These early humans acquired the use of fire and they clothed themselves to protect against the elements. They began to farm and store food. Then, once they had become acquainted with all the useful things in life, they made civilization happen:

> The arts and whatever else is capable of furthering man's social life were gradually discovered. Indeed, ... in all things it was necessity itself that became man's teacher, supplying in appropriate fashion instruction in every matter to a creature which was well endowed by nature and had, as its assistants for every purpose, hands and speech and sagacity of mind.[5]

What an original, forward-looking story—this narrative of creation developed in what sounds to us like real spacetime, everything transforming slowly, continuously, bit by bit. There is no mention of a supernatural or transcendent entity, no discourse with gods, no dialogue with demons. There is no who nor why in this creation myth. The ideas that hold the story together seem to anticipate the modern theory of evolution. Though lacking any element of what we would call deep time, the story makes sense to the modern scientific-minded reader. The language sounds very familiar: "since anything of such a nature"; "by reason of its lightness"; "by reason of the warmth"; "the ordered form in which it is now seen"; "attained their full development." This is the language of science, an inquiry rooted in formulating explanations based on careful observation, guided by a rational set of processes that gradually leads up to a reason for the universe we experience today. Here is a way of knowing the world that charts out a detailed sequence of related events, revealing in the seeds of one the outcome of the next—what scientists call cause and effect.

Throughout this book I have tried to demonstrate that no story of creation can truly be understood without knowing something about the experience and the environment of the storyteller—what I have called the landscape. This is what fires the storyteller's imagination. So who was this person who first put listeners in a frame of mind to embrace nature and humanity by imagining a universe that exists solely for its own sake? Who first encouraged them to develop a creative process that links precise observation with pure reason?

We know that Diodorus was born and raised in the mountainous town of Agira on the island of Sicily in the shadow of Mount Etna—a place that harbors none of the soft clay and marshy wetland that, according to the story, made up the primeval world. Just as I have been recounting his story centuries after he lived, Diodorus spun his tale from fragmented writings of the Greek geographer and historian Hecataeus, who was as distant from him in time as is Galileo from a contemporary historian writing about the founder of modern astronomy. Hecataeus lived in Miletus, a Greek colonial city situated on the west coast of Anatolia (now Turkey). He, in turn, obtained his sixth-century BCE version of answers to creation's basic

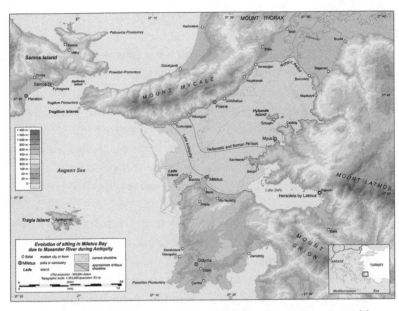

Silting in Miletus Bay at the time of the Greek creation story told
by Diodorus. *Archaic:* eighth to sixth centuries BCE; *Hellenistic:*
third to first centuries BCE; *Late Antiquity:* fourth century CE.
(Eric Gaba, Wikimedia Commons user Sting / CC BY-SA)

questions from contemporary Milesian thinkers like Anaxi-
mander, Anaximenes, and their teacher Thales, founder of the
so-called Ionian (or Milesian) school of philosophers.

You cannot begin to understand the basis for this creation story without a close-up examination of the geology and
geography of Miletus. Today the ruins of the city lie two miles
inland from the coast, but in antiquity the thriving colony possessed a bustling harbor. Alluvium brought down from the
western mountains by the Maenander River was rapidly filling
the harbor with silt, however, which by Roman times would
lead to the city's economic downfall and eventual abandon-
ment. In Hecataeus's day the coastline was extending outward

into the sea at the rate of approximately one mile per century—
enough to be easily noticeable in an average human lifetime.
Though most ancient historians thought there was little evi-
dence of any continuing change in the geology of our planet,
it seems likely that the developmental view of the natural environment that runs throughout Diodorus's narrative was influenced by the rapid changes in the landscape taking place before the eyes of the careful nature watchers who lived on it
2,500 years ago. Whirling winds, muddy potters' clay, and warm
moist swamps that churn up multitudes of living creatures
along a coastline creeping toward the Aegean—these were all
very real phenomena to the citizens of Miletus.

To understand the story's skepticism about supernatural
forces, we need to know something about its original teller.
Hecataeus is most well-known for his writings on geography,
which included the first map of the world. Centered on the
watery domain of the Mediterranean and the Aegean, the map
consisted of Europe, Western Asia, and northern Africa, all of
it encircled by an ocean—a world sensibly envisioned by one
living at the edge of a peninsula. Though only fragments of his
writings remain, Hecataeus reports many stories told to him
in his travels by Persian, Egyptian, and Indian elites regarding
their descent from the gods through multiple generations. Skep-
tical of the trustworthiness of these oral accounts, he seems to
have honed a dubious attitude overall.

The Ionian worldview was a radical departure from the
norm at the time, but the century that followed seemed ripe
for an intellectual revolution. After a long period of domina-
tion by the Persians, in 490 BCE the Greeks sacked their eastern
foe in the Battle of Marathon, opening a new era of freedom.
Now they could turn their thoughts to expansions of their
own, to advancing trade and commerce—and to probing and
contemplating the workings of a much bigger world than the

tumultuous one that had previously preoccupied them. Without the distractions of war, Greek society acquired the luxury of "thought time" to wonder how the world beneath and around them was constructed, and what makes the stars move across the sky. This is the world into which the radical ideas of the Milesian philosophers were thrust. And so Hecataeus, and later Diodorus, pass on to us a creation story based on a practical way of thinking about the origin of the wider environment. The central character in their tale is no god, no heroic dynasty, but a stable, water-borne world teeming with life in the midst of a rich, nurturing sea—all of it governed by self-contained principles.

Can you detect any similarities in this creation story, told 2,500 years later?

> Long ago a star formed in a vast cloud or nebula. It happened when a uniform mixture of gases and grainy particles separated out and condensed as a result of mutual forces of attraction inherent in all forms of matter. The energy acquired from this gathering caused the star to give off light and heat. Over a long period, the squeezing together of this nebulous matter also took place in various portions of the cloud surrounding the star, creating planets. As these smaller condensations rolled in continual motion in orbits of varying size about the central star, clumps of matter stuck together, like so many sticky snowballs rolling downhill. The planets cooled off, with the smaller among them developing hard surfaces overlain by lighter oceans topped with even lighter atmospheres that formed due to the upward movement of lighter materials in the interior. The

central star heated further, which caused much of
the gaseous material from the planets closest to it
to be driven off into space. It also created the proper
heating conditions to induce chemical reactions that
changed the composition of each atmosphere. Because of the gradual process of change, the atmo-
spheres of the planets became quite different from
one another, as verified by observations with earth-
based telescopes and imagery from interplanetary
probes. It was in the warm oceans beneath a nurturing temperate atmosphere on one of these worlds
that life gradually developed.[6]

You can find that creation story in any source on contemporary cosmology.

Notes

Prologue

1. F. Jabr, "The Story of Storytelling," *Harper's* 338 (March 2019): 35–41.

2. A. Watts, quoted in C. Long, *Alpha: The Myths of Creation* (New York: Braziller, 1963), xiii.

3. A. Aveni, *Star Stories: Constellations and People* (New Haven: Yale University Press, 2019).

4. Among the compilations and classifications of world myth from the study of religions, I recommend the works of C. Long, as well as B. Sproul, *Primal Myths: Creation Myths Around the World* (San Francisco: Harper and Row, 1979), and D. Leeming, *Creation Myths of the World: An Encyclopedia,* 2nd ed. (Santa Barbara, CA: ABC-CLIO, 2010).

5. The interdisciplinary work of D. Carrasco is a notable exception. See, for example, *Aztec Ceremonial Landscapes* (Boulder: University Press of Colorado, 1991), in which Carrasco focuses on primarily these ceremonial landscapes—landscapes marked, mapped, and rejuvenated by complex sets of performances that communicate knowledge about social and symbolic order and its sacred foundations.

6. C. Jung and C. Kerényi, *Essays on a Science of Mythology,* trans. R. Hull (Princeton: Princeton University Press, 1949), 101. More popularly known in the Jungian school is Joseph Campbell, who has developed the idea of the monomyth, or hero's journey, in which a narrator in crisis is transformed following a great adventure that ends in a victory; see P. Cousineau, ed., *The Hero's Journey: Joseph Campbell on His Life and Work* (New York: Harper, 1990). See also M. von Franz, *Creation Myths* (Boulder, CO: Shambhala, 2001).

7. I agree with Mary Barnard, whose example I refer to here. As she puts

it so well: "But isn't this putting Medea's chariot before her team of serpents?" M. Barnard, *The Mythmakers* (Athens: Ohio University Press, 1966), 21.

8. I know of few texts on myth and real-world landscape. Among those I can recommend are M. Egeler, *Landscape and Myth in North-Western Europe* (Turnhout, Belgium: Brepols, 2019); and G. Hawes, ed., *Myths on the Map: The Storied Landscapes of Ancient Greece* (Oxford: Oxford University Press, 2017). There are also a number of texts on popular creation myths, largely directed toward children, that emphasize landscape. Among these I can recommend D. Anderson, *The Origin of Life on Earth: An African Creation Myth* (Mt. Airy, MD: Sights, 1991); V. Hamilton, *In the Beginning: Creation Stories from Around the World* (Boston: Houghton Mifflin, 1988); and D. Hofmeyr, *The Star-Bearer* (London: Frances Lincoln, 2012).

Introduction

1. All biblical quotations are taken from *The New Oxford Annotated Bible with the Apocrypha*, exp. ed., ed. H. May and B. Metzger (New York: Oxford University Press, 1977). The designation "Yahweh Alone" was taken from M. Smith, *Palestinian Parties and Politics That Shaped the Old Testament* (New York: SCM Press, 1971). Historian of religion Charles Long thinks it incorrect to conclude that there is a natural development from the worship of multiple nature deities to monotheism, and asserts that we need not think of the worship of a single supreme being, the defining characteristic of the Semitic religions, as the apex of the history of religions. See his *Alpha: The Myths of Creation* (New York: Braziller, 1963), 148.

2. Once again I am indebted to M. Barnard, here regarding "the food of mythic knowledge." See Barnard, *Mythmakers* (Athens: Ohio University Press, 1966), 21.

3. The scientific study of waves referred to in the parting of the Red Sea is by D. Nof and N. Paldor, "Are There Oceanographic Explanations for the Israelites' Crossing of the Red Sea?" *Bulletin of the American Meteorological Society* 73, no. 3 (1992): 305–315.

4. M. Buber, *Moses: The Revelation and the Covenant* (New York: Harper's, 1946), 75.

5. The modern Big Bang theory's predecessor is the primeval atom or cosmic egg theory proposed in a 1946 work by the Belgian priest Georges Lemaître: *L'hypothèse de l'atome primitif: essai de cosmogonie* (Brussels: Griffon, 1946).

6. S. Weinberg, *The First Three Minutes* (New York: Basic Books, 1988), 154.

7. The multiple agents and processes of creation outlined in this chapter are well summarized in D. Leeming, *Creation Myths Around the World* (Santa Barbara, CA: ABC-CLIO, 2010), 2–29.

8. On layered universes, see my essay "Where Orbits Came From and How the Greeks Unstacked the Deck," in A. Aveni, *Uncommon Sense: Understanding Nature's Truths Across Time and Culture* (Boulder: University Press of Colorado, 2006), ch. 2. For more on landscapes, see J. Christie, ed., *Landscapes of Origin in the Americas: Creation Narratives Linking Ancient Places and Present Communities* (Tuscaloosa: University of Alabama Press, 2009).

1

Power Politics on Mount Olympus

Part 1 opener: The idea that the land makes us live right comes from elder Mrs. Annie Peaches, as told to anthropologist Keith Basso in "'Stalking with Stories': Names, Places, and Moral Narratives Among the Western Apache," in E. Bruner, ed., *Text, Play, and Story: The Construction and Reconstruction of Self and Society* (Washington, D.C.: American Ethnological Society, 1983), 19–55, quotation on 20. I acknowledge T. Griffin-Pierce for raising this point in "The Hooghan and the Stars," in R. Williamson and C. Farrer, eds., *Earth and Sky: Visions of the Cosmos in Native American Folklore* (Albuquerque: University of New Mexico Press, 1992), 110–130, see esp. 111–112. The quotation from the "earthquake child" is from "Born Among the Dead," Vice News video, available at https://www.vice.com/en_us/article/qbxzy7/born -amongst-the-dead-meeting-the-children-of-mexico-citys-tragic-1985 -earthquake-876, accessed August 6, 2020.

1. Reference to Mount Olympus as the "threshold" appears in, among other places, the *Iliad* 1.591, wherein Hephaistos, God of Fire, in a dispute in the Palace of Zeus, is grabbed by the toe and thrown down from the heavenly threshold by the king of the gods.

2. On *Theogony* and related works, see M. West, *Hesiod: Theogony* (Oxford: Oxford University Press, 1966).

3. The Greeks believed that the Mycenaean kings were their ancestors and therefore must have belonged to the heroic period of Greek mythology, when the Theban and Trojan wars were won. Technically they are the first Greeks in the sense that they were first to speak the Greek language. Their civilization thrived on the Peloponnese, Greece's southern peninsula, between 1650 and 1250 BCE. The ruins of the impressive Bronze Age Temple of Mycenae must have impressed the Greek historians who would write of their ancestors centuries later.

4. Hesiod, *Theogony*, in R. M. Frazer, trans., *The Poems of Hesiod* (Norman: University of Oklahoma Press, 1983), 156–163.

5. Ibid., 822–830.

6. Ibid., 855–862. An identification of Aidna with a specific place in the landscape surrounding Mount Olympus has yet to be agreed on. Frazer suggests it was later equated with Mount Etna in Sicily, but Hesiod more likely located it somewhere in Asia Minor.

7. Ibid., 174–175.

2
How China Got Its Tilted Landscape

1. The principal source of the version of the Pan Gu (also called P'an Ku) myth I have adopted is from the Shenyun Performing Arts website; see shenyunperformingarts.org/explore/category/chinese-stories-history, accessed July 14, 2020. The story comes from Daoist author Xu Zheng and was derived from the Zhou dynasty (first millennium BCE). I have also drawn material on Nu Wa (also called NüWa) from A. Friedman and M. Johnson, "Nu Wa's Ways (A Chinese Legend)," *Tell Me a Story* (Cambridge Universal Press Syndicate, 1992).

2. Mount Buzhou is said to be the northwest pillar that held up the sky. Though largely mythical, it is thought to be located among the Pamir Mountains in Central Asia (today Tajikistan).

3
The Four Sides of the Navajo Universe

1. For more on the celestial imagery in *Diné Bahane'* see my *People and the Sky: Our Ancestors and the Cosmos* (London: Thames and Hudson, 2008), ch. 1.

2. R. Louis, *Child of the Hogan* (Provo, UT: Brigham Young University Press, 1975), 3.

3. Concerning holes in the world, the *sipapu*, or hole found in the center of the floors of sunken Anasazi *kivas* (ceremonial rooms), reminds us of the openings from which the ancestors emerged from the other worlds.

4. P. Zolbrod, *Diné Bahane': The Navajo Creation Story* (Albuquerque: University of New Mexico Press, 1984), 35–36.

5. Ibid., 38.

6. Ibid., 41.

7. Ibid., 42.

8. Ibid., 58.

9. Ibid., 82.

10. Many readers will have heard of Wile E. Coyote ("wily"), a cartoon character who spends most of his time chasing, but never catching, his quarry, the Road Runner. He builds complex contraptions that backfire and repeatedly misses sharp turns while engaged in the chase, often finding himself in mid-air off the edge of a cliff. Once he recognizes his impossible condition he suddenly becomes aware of the law of gravity, which sends him plunging to the desert floor in a cloud of dust. The comical coyote's slapstick actions have merited Wile E. Coyote a place among a national magazine's list of "The 60 Nastiest Villains of All Time" (listal.com/list/tv-guides-60-nastiest-villains, accessed July 14, 2020). Coyotes acquired their lasting negative image of being cowardly and untrustworthy from the first European settlers in America, who blamed them, often unjustly, for attacks on deer, turkey, and domesticated animals. Western North Americans especially loathe coyotes for the damage they do to their livestock. (Actually, the wolf deserves the bulk of the blame.) Rarely seen, and then only seeming to skulk about—their tails between their legs—coyotes make their presence known to us by their penetrating, high-pitched howl. But those who study canid species find coyotes quite intelligent, versatile, and adaptable animals. Unlike wolves, they are monogamous, with the male helping in raising the pups. They are more like humans than any animals confronted by native dwellers of the southwest, which probably accounts for their central role in Navajo creation stories. Why a Trickster? We think of a trickster as one who uses deception laced with a bit of humor to rebel against social conventions. That the coyote is primarily a scavenger rather than a predator makes him a cunning carnivore—one who compensates for his small size by being smart. And coyotes' cleverness and adaptability make them difficult to trap and therefore hard to eradicate. Typically, coyotes follow larger carnivores, waiting for the opportunity to snatch a piece of the catch; for example, after a bear has caught an animal, a coyote might dart in and nip the larger predator in the leg. When the startled and confused bear momentarily drops his meal, the coyote will quickly make off with it. The scene is actually quite comical: the ferocious monster is outdone by a wily subordinate. If you watch a lot of their behavior you might come to believe that coyotes have a sense of humor. See, e.g., W. Robinson, "Some Observations on Coyote Predation in Yellowstone National Park," *Journal of Mammalogy* 33, no. 4 (1947): 470–476. The coyote-trickster profile has even found a place in the biological species nomenclature: *Canis latrans frustror* (tricky coyote); and *Canis latrans cagottis*

(cagey coyote), *clepticus* (thieving), *impavidus* (undauntable), and *vigilis* (alert)—all adjectives that suggest how coyotes have annoyed western ranchers both ancient and modern.

11. P. Schaafsma, "Human Images and Blurring Boundaries: The Pueblo Body in Cosmological Context; Rock Art, Murals and Ceremonial Figures," *Cambridge Archaeological Journal* 28, no. 3 (2018), 411–431, displays in pictorial rather than narrative form the same sort of depictions of humanity conflated with other life forms and cosmological entities that are described in *Diné Bahane'*.

4
Five Aztec Creations

1. The Aztec story of the Five Suns is recounted in sixteenth-century Fray Bernardino de Sahagún's *Florentine Codex: General History of the Things of New Spain*, trans. A. Anderson and C. Dibble, books 3 and 7, Monographs of the School of American Research, Santa Fe, 1978 and 1953, respectively. See especially *Book 7: The Sun, Moon, and Stars, and the Binding of the Years*, pp. 4–8, from which all passages herein are quoted.

5
Creation Battles in the Andean Highlands

1. J. Murra, "El control vertical de un máximo de pisos ecológicos en la economía de las sociedades andinas," in J. Murra, ed., *Vista de la Provincia de Leon de Huánuco*, vol. 2 (Huánuco, Peru: Universidad Hermilio Valdizán, 1972), 429–476.

2. Unlike the Aztec creation story, wherein the gods destroy unsatisfactory versions of the world, in the Andean myth a dissatisfied world sees fit to destroy itself. In both cases, the world *is* the gods: Paria Caca is the Storm, Nanauatzin the Sun. But keep in mind that the Aztec myth is the product of a militaristic empire that looks to a powerful natural force to propagate its existence, while the highly animated Andean story is told by a class of peasants who live their lives in closer contact with nature.

3. "Baked Potato Gleaner" or simply "Potato Eater" is an ideal moniker for the outer garb of Huatya Curi: he dresses in rags and looks just like the potato: ugly on the outside (like our Aztec hero Nanauatzin), with bumps, discoloration, and white protuberances—but nourishing on the inside. This

original staple food of the Andes would later sustain much of the rest of the world.

4. F. Salomon and G. Urioste, trans. and ed., *The Huarochirí Manuscript: A Testament of Ancient and Colonial Andean Religion* (Austin: University of Texas Press, 1991), 56. The original manuscript, dated ca. 1600, was compiled by the Jesuit priest Francisco de Ávila and is based on the information acquired via his native informant, one Cristóbal Choquecasa. (That Paria Caca sends his son to change the world may be a Christian intrusion.)

5. Ibid., 57–58.

6. Ibid., 58.

7. Ibid., 59.

8. On lithification, literally getting turned into stone, see J. Dulanto, "Time and the Other: The Early Colonial Mythohistorical Landscapes of the Huarochirí Manuscript," in A. Aveni, ed., *The Measure and Meaning of Time in Mesoamerica and the Andes* (Washington, DC: Dumbarton Oaks Center for Pre-Columbian Studies, 2015), ch. 8. There Dulanto has mapped the up and down route of confrontation between Paria Caca and Huallallo Caruincho, locating in the actual landscape many of the huacas mentioned in the story.

9. Salomon and Urioste, *Huarochirí Manuscript*, 59.

10. For more on Andean mythology, see G. Urton, *Inca Myths* (Austin: University of Texas Press, 1999). On complementary dualism, see R. Harrison, *Signs, Songs, and Memory in the Andes: Translating Quechuan Language and Culture* (Austin: University of Texas Press, 1989).

6
Salt of the Earth

1. Wrapped around this tale about the uses and misuses of power is the idea of mental cartography—a classification system of the minerals in the landscape used by Fernando Santos-Granero, a research scientist and anthropologist at the Smithsonian Tropical Research Institute in Panama. His telling of the story, one of many acquired from Southern Arawak elders, is briefly recounted here. See F. Santos-Granero, "Arawakan Sacred Landscapes. Emplaced Myths, Place Rituals, and the Production of Locality of Western Amazonia," in E. Halbmayer and E. Mader, eds., *Kultur, Raum, Landschaft. Zur Bedeutung des Raumes in Zeiten der Globalität* (Frankfurt: Brandes and Apsel Verlag, 2004), 93–122.

7
Enuma Elish

1. The recitation of *Enuma Elish* took place at the time of the seasonal renewal of life—the Akitu Festival of the Babylonian New Year. From a religious standpoint, proclaiming the power of the gods exorcised evil by ridding the temple of negative forces. But there also existed a patriotic rationale. In the second part of the creation story a patrilineal military state replaces the matrilineal agricultural one from the first part. This dramatization of the powerful present world order was designed to cultivate devotion to Marduk, king of all the gods, and to offer some assurance of a favorable destiny for the land the people inhabited—excellent political propaganda. Afraid of a volatile climate capable of threatening them with starvation coupled with threats posed by invaders from the north, the people needed an authoritarian force like Marduk to sustain them. Like the celestial bodies that renewed their appearance at the end of each appointed round, the people celebrating Akitu appealed to Marduk in the hope of assuring continuation of the good life— at least for another year. But let's not underestimate the power of the ecological thread that holds *Enuma* together—especially if we think of its recitation as a magic formula concocted to combat the inundation that happens every spring following the snow melt in the mountains of Armenia and Kurdistan. "May he subdue Tiamat, may he distress her life, and may it be short!" reads a line in the final tablet, a reminder of the threat of floods, which imitate the primordial chaos when the turbulent waters once were present everywhere. (See A. Heidel, *The Babylonian Genesis*, 2nd ed. [Chicago: University of Chicago Press, 1951], tablet 7, line 132.) One of the environmental triumphs of the great city of Marduk was the construction of irrigation channels that helped tame the flood. When the story was first written down, Babylon lay close to the Persian Gulf. Just as the land on which it was built grew from year to year by silt deposits carried down to the gulf by the rivers, so too the earth came about in *Enuma Elish*. The earliest hint of the seasonal holiday we call Easter/Passover descends from the twenty-fourth-century BCE Babylonian Akitu festival. First celebrated in the Mesopotamian city of Ur, located in southern Iraq, it was dedicated to the moon and the equinoxes. The Babylonians recognized two six-month half-years, or semesters, each with its own moon feast, celebrated on the first and seventh months and marked by full moons Nisannu (March/April) and Tasritu (September/October). During the period of Babylonian captivity (sixth century BCE), the ancient Hebrews picked up the idea of the equinoxes as the turning points of the year: "You should observe the Feast of Weeks, of the first fruits of the wheat harvest, and the Feast of the Ingather-

ing at the turn of the year," reads Exodus 34:22. The Feast of the Unleavened Bread at the turn of the year, when the kings do battle, came to be tied to the first of the two holidays, which was emphasized in particular by the Israelites. When Moses received instructions from Yahweh that the Israelites were to flee captivity by the light of the full moon, he told each family to sacrifice a lamb and sprinkle its blood over the doorjamb as a sign to the angel who would pass over their homes not to kill their firstborn. In haste they would be forced to bring unleavened bread with them to sustain their long journey. Setting the date of the feast turned out to be a complex problem that would occupy calendar keepers for centuries. (For a detailed account, see my *Book of the Year: A Brief History of the Seasonal Holidays* [Oxford: Oxford University Press, 2003], ch. 5.) Despite profound differences, e.g., monotheism versus polytheism and creation by word versus creation by action, some scholars find parallels between *Enuma Elish* and the later Old Testament: a watery chaos separated into heaven and earth, the etymological equivalence in names denoting the chaos, and the existence of light prior to creation. Furthermore, there are seven tablets (one-fourth of a lunar phase cycle)—the same as the number of days of creation in the Hebraic account.

2. A. Heidel, *The Babylonian Genesis,* 2nd ed. (Chicago: University of Chicago Press, 1951) is the source used here. The earliest version of *Enuma Elish* dates from the First Dynasty of the Babylonian empire (ca. 1830 BCE). In describing its principal hero Marduk, King of the Gods, who would later become Zeus in the Greek and Jupiter in the Roman pantheon, Babylon's most famous king, Hammurabi, would state in his Code of Laws (the oldest laws in written history): "When the God Marduk commanded me to provide just ways for the people of the land (in order to attain) appropriate behavior, I established truth and justice as the declaration of the land (and) I enhanced the well-being of the people." See J. Unterman, *Justice for All: How the Jewish Bible Revolutionized Ethics* (Philadelphia: Jewish Publication Society, 2017), 20. When Hammurabi stated this at the height of his power (ca. 1760 BCE), he had gained control, by military force, of the entire Tigris-Euphrates valley from the Zagros mountains in the north of today's Iraq all the way to the Persian Gulf. He also had tamed the annual floods by undertaking massive irrigation projects. In the history of the dynasty passed down to us, Hammurabi becomes the in-the-flesh version of Marduk, who triumphs over nature by force.

3. Heidel, *Babylonian Genesis,* tablet 1, line 16.

4. Ibid., tablet 1, line 45.

5. Ibid., tablet 4, lines 97–103.

6. Ibid., tablet 4, lines 137–140.

7. Ibid., tablet 5, lines 2–14.

8. For "not suited to human understanding," ibid., tablet 4, line 37. "Workers needed" is the term used by E. Wasilewska in her *Creation Stories of the Middle East* (London: Jessica Kingsley, 2000). For a more detailed discussion of themes discussed here, I recommend especially pp. 87–90. See also M. Coogan, *Ancient Near Eastern Texts* (Oxford: Oxford University Press, 2012), 144. For "imposed the services of the gods," see Heidel, *Babylonian Genesis,* tablet 6, line 34.

8
The Nile from Benben to Pyramid

1. A Gardiner, *Egyptian Grammar* (Oxford: Oxford University Press, 1957), 3rd ed.

2. Located in Lower Egypt at the southern end of the Nile River delta, Heliopolis was the cult center of the sun deity Atum, later Ra (Re), early in the third millennium BCE. All four basic variants of Egyptian creation (the Heliopolitan—told here—the Hermopolitan, the Memphite, and the Theban, after their cities of origin) share in the idea of creation as an ongoing process. For a detailed comparison, see E. Wasilewska, *Creation Stories of the Middle East,* esp. 58–60 and 144–146. Interestingly, in the Egyptian version of creation, earth is male and sky female—the opposite of what we find in most creation stories.

3. J. Wilson, "Egyptian Mortuary Texts, Myths, and Tales," in J. Pritchard, ed., *Ancient Near Eastern Texts Relating to the Old Testament* (Princeton: Princeton University Press, 1950), 6–7.

4. Think of the pairings: good-evil, sun-moon, gold-silver, male-female. Life has its ups and downs, its love-hate relationships, and everyone has heard that you need to experience pain to appreciate pleasure. Do we define our emotions to reflect extremes that are part of a continuous spectrum, or do we think of them as polar opposites: grief and joy, depression and elation? I think we structure nature exactly the way we structure sensibilities. This is why mythology sometimes portrays planets in pairs (or dyads) and at other times splits them in half—literally regarding them as two separable, opposing yet complementary entities (or moieties). We find this sort of dualistic arrangement recurring in many myths—especially those involving twins. Also, recall the vertical dualism in Andean mythology. One of the best illustrations of dyadic structure from Western mythology involves the two aspects of Venus, the Goddess of Love. Her morning and evening celestial attitudes personified all the love and hate a human being could imagine rolled into one bright white light. Finally, note that our word *hermaphrodite* (Her-

mes plus Aphrodite), is a combination of the Greek names for Mercury and Venus.

5. Some readers have noted the resonance between the sudden cataclysmic creation event in many versions of Egyptian creation and the modern Big Bang Theory, which also calls for a merging—though in a much more abstract vein, with neutrons resulting from the collision of electrons and protons. In my view the resemblance is superficial. As we have already learned, merging as well as separating, not to mention cataclysm, are forms of action shared by many cosmogonies from a variety of world cultures.

6. B. Sproul, *Primal Myths: Creation Myths Around the World* (San Francisco: Harper, 1979), 89. The *Pyramid Texts*, taken from tomb walls, coffins, and scrolls, ca. 2600–2100 BCE, are the primary source of stories of creation from Egypt. Material in these relatively late texts resonates with fragments of myths dated two thousand years earlier. Modern references and compilations include F. Fleming and A. Lothian, *The Way to Eternity: Egyptian Myth* (Amsterdam: Time-Life, 1997), 23–42; J. Allen, *The Ancient Pyramid Texts* (*Writings from the Ancient World*) (Atlanta: Society of Biblical Literature, 2015); and A. Johnson Hodari and Y. McCalla Sobers, *Lifelines: The Black Book of Proverbs* (New York: Broadway, 2009).

7. On the Shilluk myth, see P. Freund, *Myths of Creation* (New York: Washington Square Press, 1965), 6.

9
The Mande and the River Niger

1. The baobab tree stars in a number of African creation stories. For example, the Yoruba creator god makes the soil of earth fertile by dusting it with baobab powder. All shaman live near it and gather things that grow around it to place in their divining tray. See D. Anderson, *The Origin of Life on Earth: An African Creation Myth* (Mt. Airy, MD: Sights, 1991).

2. Mande (Mandé) is actually a language-related set of ethnic people spanning a large portion of West Africa from Niger and Nigeria to the south and west coast.

3. G. Dieterlen, "The Mande Creation Myth," *Africa: Journal of the International African Institute* 27, no. 2 (1957): 137.

4. Ibid., 126.

5. Ibid., 128. Following the first rainstorm, two stars were said to be seen circling Sirius. They represented the twin descents of the seeds, one symbolizing Pemba's male seeds, the other Faro's female seeds. The connection between twinness by descent tied to Sirius and the fact, established in 1862,

that Sirius has a faint companion not visible without a telescope has been taken by some investigators to imply that West African people, especially the Dogon, who belong to the same linguistic group, had acquired such extraordinary knowledge from extraterrestrial beings. I think it's more likely the scientific aspects of Sirius's makeup came from Jesuit missionaries who communicated with these people. There are other cross-cultural intrusions that affect the story line. Recall the seminal role of the observation of Sirius in the Nile seasonal inundation. Judeo-Christian influence is obvious in the ark, but the flood episode is connected to the river and the indigenous element of twinness is retained.

10

Tlingit Origins

1. J. Teit, "Tahltan Tales," *Journal of American Folklore* 32 (1919): 198–250. The amalgam of stories selected for this chapter comes from a collection of twenty-nine myths told by Tlingit elders that make up part of the Tlingit Raven Cycle. The image of Raven characterized by Tlingit storytellers is well earned. Technological skills of the raven include fashioning bits of twigs to probe holes in trees in search of insect larvae. With a two-foot-long average wingspan, their aerobatic flying—sometimes upside down—can be very impressive. Ravens are confident, inquisitive, and above all, clever predators. For example, one member of a hunting pair (they mate for life) will often distract an incubating adult prey while the other sneaks in and snatches an egg from the nest. They have been observed mimicking bird calls and flying in the direction of the sound of gunshots in anticipation of locating a carcass. Ravens also distract wolves who have just opened a carcass by calling out to them and directing them to lesser game so that they can steal the remains. Some have even been observed making caches without depositing food in order to confuse onlookers. The raven description is taken from L. Weber and J. Weber, *Nature Watch Big Bend: A Seasonal Guide* (College Station: Texas A&M University Press, 2017), 19. For further resources, I recommend the website of the Central Council of the Tlingit and Haida Indian Tribes of Alaska (ccthita.org, accessed July 14, 2020). Artistic renditions of the myth can be found in the blog of Preston Singletary at prestonsingletary.com, accessed July 14, 2020.

2. Teit, "Tahltan Tales," 205. The impregnation of the young daughter is often regarded as a Christian intrusion—the immaculate conception. I am not so sure. The question of the origin of pregnancy arises in creation myths

from a variety of cultures; one logical way of explaining it might be via oral ingestion of some magical substance. The same opinion holds for the flood story, which is often relegated to the biblical flood myth. But I think it may be of local origin. The dramatic rise and fall of the sea along the west coast of the United States and Canada happens during tsunamis primarily caused by Alaskan earthquakes. See D. Vitaliano, "Geomythology: Geological Origins of Myths and Legends," in L. Piccardi and W. Masse, eds., *Myth and Geology* (London: Geological Society Special Publications 273, 2007), 1–7.

3. Teit, "Tahltan Tales," 201–202.

4. Ibid., 206.

5. Ibid., 201–202.

6. Ibid., 202.

7. Ibid., 202–203.

11

A Dreamtime Creation from Southwest Australia

Part 3 opener: I am grateful for the analogy of the dead tree example of transformation, which is from B. Sproul, *Primal Myths: Creation Myths Around the World* (San Francisco: Harper, 1979), 22.

1. See, e.g., C. Berndt, "Mythology," in D. Horton, ed., *The Encyclopedia of Aboriginal Australia: Aboriginal and Torres Strait Islander History, Society and Culture* (Canberra: Aboriginal Studies Press, 1994).

2. The first printed version of this story appears in W. Smith, *Myths and Legends of the Australian Aborigines* (New York: Farrar and Rinehart, 1932), 23–40. Indigenous Australian people have rightly pointed out that books written about the subject of Aborigines have been authored by white people, who tend to write in terms of their own ways of knowing, thus giving too little consideration of reality as it might appear to the indigenous narrator. For a critique of the Dreamtime literature, I recommend the 2000 Adelaide University dissertation of Mary-Anne Gale: "Poor Bugger Whitefella Got No Dreaming: The Representation and Appropriation of Published Dreaming Narratives with Special Reference to David Unaipon's Writings," in *Legendary Tales of the Australian Aborigines*, repr. ed. (Melbourne: Melbourne University Press, 2001). One of Gale's contentions is that the landscape—the very subject I wish to emphasize—often goes unmentioned in such literature. She also points out that parts of these narratives clearly exhibit Christian overtones. (See esp. ch. 6 of her work.) For more on the role of landscape in the myth, see A. Howitt, *The Native Tribes of South-East Australia*

(London: Macmillan, 1904), 426–434. On the particular myth told here, see also D. Wolkstein, *Sun Mother Wakes the World: An Australian Creation Story* (New York: HarperCollins), 2004.

3. The name derives from the name of the people of South Australia who worship her. Alternative names, such as Dietyi or Yhi, apply in southeast Australia. On the meaning of the place Killa-wilpa-nina (*killa* means vagina, while *wilpa* means hole), see Howitt, *Native Tribes,* 427, n. 6. Many Australian caves have yet to be fully explored. In 1988, fifteen members of a cave-diving expedition became trapped underground in one of the Nullarbor caves when a cyclone produced a rainstorm that led to a two-meter (six-foot) surge of water.

4. Smith, *Myths and Legends,* 36.

5. While the creative forces in most stories told in Australia come from the west, the side of the continent that faces Southeast Asia and the source of migration since the last Ice Age, the people of southwest Australia speak of those who came down from above. Though features of the local landscape are clearly discernible and much of the action takes place below, specifically in the abundant caves, some of the elements of the story may be influenced by Christian colonizers; for example, the voice from on high resounding over a hilltop on which the first people and animals assemble, and the idea of people having dominion over animals. The swirling dust pillars likely refer to sandstorms that come down from the Great Victoria Desert to the north.

12
An Underworld Battle and the Maya Dawn of Life

1. The Quiché Maya, who occupy the rainforest of the Petén region of northern Guatemala, say that *Popol Vuh,* of which only a copy produced in colonial times survives, tells what happened when their ancestors, the Quiché lords who established the great Maya civilization of Yucatán, undertook a pilgrimage from their mountain highland home to the Caribbean. Along the way they discovered a book that told what happened before the first dawn and their ancestors' encounter with the spirits of their gods in the forests. They called it the Book of the Dawn of Life. Dated to 100 BCE, the San Bartolo mural paintings from the rainforest of northern Guatemala depict a scene highly reminiscent of scenes from the *Popol Vuh,* among them a corn baby held by a man kneeling in water, and a maize deity in a turtle-shaped cave dancing before a pair of enthroned water deities. That the divine right to rule emanates from the gods is supported by the image of a king imper-

sonating the hero Hunahpu, who makes a divine sacrificial blood offering by piercing his penis with a spear.

2. D. Tedlock, *Popol Vuh: The Definitive Edition of the Mayan Book of the Dawn of Life and the Glories of Gods and Kings,* rev. and exp. ed. (1985; New York: Simon and Schuster, 1996).

3. See, e.g., my *Skywatchers of Ancient Mexico,* rev. ed. (Austin: University of Texas Press, 2001), esp. ch. 4.

4. I also recommend A. Christenson, *Popol Vuh: The Sacred Book of the Maya* (Norman: University of Oklahoma Press, 2003).

5. Tedlock, *Popol Vuh,* 63.

6. Ibid., 65.

7. Ibid., 67–68.

8. Ibid.

9. Ibid., 70.

10. Ibid., 132, 134–137.

11. Ibid.

12. Ibid., 138.

13
Inca Ancestors Emerge

1. References to actual places in the landscape mentioned in this brief account are well documented; for example, archaeologist Brian Bauer has identified an archaeological site located in the District of Pacariqtambo, south of Cusco, which contains remains of an oracle of the quasi-mythical first Inca king Manco Cápac. Graphic representations of the place known today as Tambo Toco that appear in the chronicles show it represented as a cave, and below the site there is an actual cave. Bauer argues that the myth is intended to show that the existing social order comes from a set of events that happened outside of normal space-time resulting from powers beyond the range of human existence—so it cannot be challenged by contemporary human action. Kin groups don't think of themselves as belonging to certain boundaries defined by the landscape. Bauer also traces the downhill route from there to Cusco, a parallel on a smaller scale to the route from Lake Titicaca. Unquestionably, the lake in the Collasuyu quadrant, one of the four sections of the world, is Lake Titicaca, which sits at an altitude of 3,800 meters (12,500 ft.), 650 kilometers (400 mi.) from Cusco, in Bolivia, close to the border of modern Peru. See B. Bauer, "Pacariqtambo and the Mythical Origins of the Inca," *Latin American Antiquity* 2, no. 1 (1991): 7–26. Another version of Inca creation promulgated by the empire has Viracocha first fash-

ioning a race of stone giants. But they were selfish and greedy, so he made humans, who also proved unsatisfactory. He sent a flood to do in the lot of them, all of this happening before he created Inti. The word "Ayar" derives from *aya,* or corpse, in the spoken Quechua language, which connects the mythological ancestors with the mummified remains of the Inca kings, which were housed for worship in the Temple of the Ancestors in Cusco.

2. Because the Inca system of writing on knotted strings has not been fully deciphered, the mythical subterranean journey of the first humans is related only in fragments from Spanish chroniclers. The account given here is from anthropologist Gary Urton's work *Inca Myths* (London: British Museum Press, 1999), 34–37 and 45–51, which was drawn largely from P. Sarmiento de Gamboa, *The History of the Incas,* trans. B. Bauer and V. Smith (1572; Austin: University of Texas Press, 2007).

14
A Creation Story from Polynesia

Part 4 opener: One such "pumice raft" spanning 150 kilometers (90 mi.) that surfaced near Fiji in 2019 was described by sailors who navigated it as a "rock rubble slick made up of pumice stones from marble to basketball size." A. Chambers, "Sailors Encounter Floating Pumice 'Raft' Drifting Across the Pacific Ocean," ABC News, August 28, 2019, abcnews.go.com/International /sailors-encounter-floating-pumice-raft-drifting-pacific-ocean/story?id =65242139, accessed July 14, 2020.

1. J. Andersen, *Myths and Legends of the Polynesians* (New York: Dover, 1995), 367. Principally of Maori origin, this story comes from an 1855 collection of Polynesian myths and legends originally published by New Zealand governor Sir George Grey (*Polynesian Mythology and Ancient Traditional History of the New Zealand Race, as Furnished by Their Priests and Chiefs,* published by John Murray in London), and credited to the writings of a Te Arawa Maori chief of northern New Zealand. Given the secondhand acquisition of the orally told story by an outsider, it isn't difficult to spot Western embellishments that lurk in the retelling, as is the case in other so-called indigenous narratives of world parent myths in this collection. For example, the children attempting to do in their parents and the sibling rivalry they display also surface in the Babylonian *Enuma Elish* and the Greek *Theogony.* But then, such familial tensions may reveal situations common in all human behavior—the love of one parent for another competing with that between parent and child. See also R. Dixon, *Oceanic Mythology* (Boston: Marshall Jones, 1916).

2. Andersen, *Myths and Legends,* 368.

3. The reference to a classification of cloud types in the myth is not surprising. Open to the ocean on all sides, New Zealand is often buffeted by strong winds and squalls, offering the discerning eye a multitude of cloud images.

4. A source of food among the Maori of New Zealand, the *whanake,* or cabbage tree, is a tree much like a palm, bearing strong, long narrow leaves arising from a single trunk.

15
How Maui Dredged Up the Hawaiian Islands

Epigraph: From the Hokulea archive, available at archive.hokulea.com/tra ditionspaao.html, accessed July 14, 2020.

1. The first version of the Maui myth is adapted from W. Westervelt, *Legends of Maui* (Honolulu: Hawaiian Gazette, 1910). In chapter 7 of my *Star Stories,* I tell about how the constellation named after his magical fishhook, popularized in Disney's 2016 movie *Moana,* commemorates his great feat of trickery. See Aveni, *Star Stories: Constellations and People* (New Haven: Yale University Press, 2019).

2. This version, with the struggling fish possibly reflecting memories of earthquake tremors, comes from J. Stimson, trans., "Tuamotuan Legends (Island of Anaa)," part 1: "The Demigods," *Bulletin* no. 148 (Honolulu: Bishop Museum, 1937).

3. The Tonga-Samoa version of the story is taken from J. Stair, "Jottings on the Mythology and Spirit-Lore of Old Samoa," *Journal of the Polynesian Society* 5 (1896): 33–57, esp. 35. For more about relationships among these myths and the detailed geography and geology of the island groups, see P. Nunn, "Fished Up or Thrown Down: The Geography of Pacific Island Origin Myths," *Annals of the Association of American Geographers* 93, no. 2 (2003): 350–364. The dichotomy between fishing up and throwing down is owed to Nunn's research, which offers an excellent example of the role of environmental detail in myth making.

16
Dobu Islanders and Palolo Worms

Epigraph: B. Malinowski, *Argonauts of the Western Pacific: An Account of Native Enterprise and Adventure in the Archipelagoes of Melanesian New Guinea*

(London: Routledge, 1922), 301–302. Bronislaw Malinowski is recognized as one of the founders of the field of anthropology; he published this work after spending a major part of his life researching the Dobu and related groups.

1. R. Fortune, *Sorcerers of Dobu: The Social Anthropology of the Dobu Islanders of the Western Pacific* (New York: Dutton, 1932).

2. S. McLean, "Stories and Cosmogonies: Imagining Creativity Beyond 'Nature' and 'Culture,'" *Current Anthropology* 24, no. 2 (2009): 213–245, esp. 217.

3. Fortune, *Sorcerers of Dobu,* 264.

4. Ibid., 259. The palolo is a spawning marine annelid seen on the surface of the sea at the southern extremity of the island chain every year following the full moon that falls between October 15 and November 15. They name the month Milamala after the worm and celebrate a new year's festival to inaugurate the yam planting season. Anthropologists have discovered that the same festival occurs a month earlier in islands to the north, two months earlier to the south, and three months earlier to the east. One curiosity about this system is that the whole territory completes a twelve- or a thirteen-month lunar cycle, and yet no given area actually counts more than ten months. For a full discussion of this unusual calendar system, see my *Empires of Time: Calendars, Clocks, and Cultures* (New York: Basic, 1989), 174–176. The "time-out" is a free-floating adjustable period tied to the occurrence in nature of a singular event that resets the calendar—the appearance of the palolo worm. This system is not so different from the way the Romans before Caesar kept time by the moon. Their months, also ten in number, began with March, the month of the equinox (the seasonal reset mechanism) and ended with the eighth, ninth, and tenth lunations, as their Latin names betray—Octo(ber), Novem(ber), Decem(ber). As for the rest of the Dobu year, following the tenth month there was a gap of two, sometimes three full moons until the next cycle. This uncounted interval corresponded to the temporal limbo when fields lay fallow—a borderland in time during which the farmers waited patiently for nature to signal the awakening of spring and thus rekindle the cycle. Although we have come to think of the solar or seasonal year as somehow categorically *correct,* such lunar-based calendars illustrate how a minimum of systematic knowledge about the passage of natural events can be organized into a complex workable system, wherein *transition* matters more than *duration.* Dobu islanders looked for events in the world around them that portended change—time's signposts to which they needed to respond in order to survive. Like the heliacal rise of Sirius that coincided with the Nile flood in Egypt, the appearance of the palolo worm became their time marker once they perceived its seasonal cyclic rhythm.

5. Fortune, *Sorcerers of Dobu,* 259.

17
How Our Islands Were Made

1. W. Aston, *Nihongi: Chronicles of Japan from the Earliest Times to AD 697*, vol. 1 (1897; London: G. Allen and Unwin, 1956), 1–34.

2. B. Sproul, *Primal Myths: Creation Myths Around the World* (San Francisco: Harper & Row, 1979), 213.

3. Ibid.

18
Haudenosaunee Island Making

1. The word Iroquois comes from the French reference to a Huron name attributed to Haudenosaunee ancestors. A derogatory term, it translates as "black snakes."

2. The tale narrated here is an amalgam of stories acquired from the files of the Iroquois Museum in Schoharie County, New York, as well as published historical sources. My major sources are "Creation: The Beginning," as told by Mohawk storyteller Kay Olan (i36466.wixsite.com/learninglong house/creation---kay-olan, accessed August 7, 2020), along with a version written in 1816 found in C. Klinck and J. Talman, eds., *Journal of Major John Norton* (Toronto: Champlain Society, 1970), 88–91. See also "Three Versions of the Iroquois Creation Story," available at the Iroquois Indian Museum website, iroquoismuseum.org, accessed July 14, 2020.

3. I have excluded versions of the story that interpret the brotherly good-evil duality in terms of God and the Devil, the latter taking the form of Satan, though at the very opening of the present narrative the Tree of Life does suggest Christian intrusion. Also, an immaculate conception is implied in the pregnancy of Sky Woman; humans are often represented as caretakers of the world; and the chief of Sky World is often mistaken for the Christian deity who empowers the good brother in the story.

4. Klinck and Talman, *Journal of Major John Norton*, secs. 3.12–3.13.

5. This story is based on the one on the website of First People of the United States and Canada—Turtle Island, available at http://firstpeople.us /FP-Html-Legends/Huron-Creation-Myth-Wyandot.html, accessed July 14, 2020. This is actually a Wyandot (Huron) source.

19
Diving in the Mud

1. The Cherokee creation story retold here was first published in J. Mooney, "Myths of the Cherokee," *19th Annual Report of the Bureau of American Ethnology,* part 1 (Washington, DC: Government Printing Office, 1897–1898), 239–240, as told by elder Ayúnini. See also *Creation Stories from Around the World,* 4th ed., July 2000, available at Bruce Railsback's Geosciences Resources website, http://railsback.org/CS/CSIndex.html, accessed August 6, 2020.

2. Origin myths told by neighboring tribes resemble the Cherokee version. For example, in the version of the Yuchi, who resided in the Tennessee River valley until late in the seventeenth century prior to migrating southward, it is the crawfish who first descends to the world ocean to dive for mud. In a matriarchal vein, Bright Star and Moon fail as sources of light. But *T'cho,* the Sun, emerges and says, "You are my children, I am your mother, I will make the light, I will shine for you." See J. Swanton, "Creek Stories," *US Bureau of American Ethnology Bulletin* 88, no. 90 (Washington, DC: Government Printing Office, 1929), 84–85. But there are significant differences. A monster invades the people. They cut off his hand and place it in a tree, but it rejoins his body and kills the tree. This is repeated until practically every tree in the forest is dead. Finally, they place the severed monster head in a cedar tree. As the blood of the beast trickles down the tree, the people know they have found Great Medicine—as was the case for the wild strawberry in the Haudenosaunee myth. The repeated reference to the number seven in the Cherokee myth as well as the origin of people through a miraculous birth may be a Western intrusion. The concept of a place down below where the seasons are reversed makes me wonder whether there is some knowledge conveyed in the story about what happens in the Southern Hemisphere. If so, it is not possible to know when such information was introduced.

20
Norse Creation

1. Here I have adapted Daniel McCoy's version of Norse creation, one among thirty-four accessible Norse myths that appear in his compilation D. McCoy, *The Viking Spirit: An Introduction to Norse Mythology and Religion* (CreateSpace Independent Publishing Platform, 2016). See also McCoy's website, "Norse Mythology for Smart People," at norse-mythology .org. Other resources include the free printable "The Beginning of Things:

Norse Creation Story," available at https://www.studenthandouts.com/00 /200004/beginning-of-things-nordic-germanic-creation-story.pdf, accessed July 14, 2020. The classic version of the story appears in thirteenth-century Icelandic historian Snorri Sturluson's *Prose Edda*. See J. Byock, ed., *The Prose Edda* (New York: Penguin, 2006).

2. The mythology of an endless winter may be related to distant memories of extreme weather events that took place in 535–536 CE, the most severe short-term cooling episode in the Northern Hemisphere. It happened when excess atmospheric dust followed either a tropical volcanic eruption or an asteroid impact. See J. Gunn, *The Years Without Summer: Tracing A.D. 536 and Its Aftermath* (Oxford: British Archaeological Reports International, 2000).

3. McCoy thinks the view in which no rebirth happens is an older pagan view, while the rebirth version comes later in the Viking age (800–1066 CE) via Christian influence. (The resemblance between Ragnarök and Christian Armageddon in the Book of Revelation is obvious.) While the Norse creation tale, ending in ultimate destruction, suggests a kind of hopelessness, McCoy suggests it may have been intended to encourage each of us to face our fate with dignity, honor, and courage, rather than remaining paralyzed and helpless in the face of disaster.

21
Arctic Inuit Creation

1. My principal resource for the stories and interviews with Inuit people are J. MacDonald, *The Arctic Sky: Inuit Astronomy, Star Lore, and Legend* (Toronto: Royal Ontario Museum and Nunavut Research Institute, 1998), esp. 260–261, and K. Rasmussen, *The People of the Polar North: A Record* (Philadelphia: Lippincott, 1908). Additional resources for this chapter include W. Thalbitzer, "The Ammassalik Eskimo: Contributions to the Ethnology of East Greenland Natives," *Meddelelser om Grønland* 39–40, no. 1 (1914); B. Saladin d'Anglure, "The Mythology of the Inuit of the Central Arctic," in *American, African, and Old European Mythologies*, ed. Y. Bonnefoy (Chicago: University of Chicago Press, 1993), 25–32; and B. Saladin d'Anglure, *Inuit Stories of Being and Rebirth: Gender, Shamanism, and the Third Sex* (Winnipeg: University of Manitoba Press, 2018), 39–56.

2. K. Rasmussen, "Intellectual Culture of the Iglulik Eskimos," *Report of the Fifth Thule Expedition*, vol. 7 (Copenhagen, 1929), 352.

3. We have seen the imagery of emergence and transformation, the economic problems incumbent upon eternal life, and the appearance of the

Raven in other North American creation myths, from where they likely were transmitted northward.

4. Rasmussen, "Intellectual Culture," 253.

5. MacDonald, *Arctic Sky*, 149, 151.

6. Ibid., 175–176.

7. Ibid., 287–288.

8. On Inuit spiritualism expressed in artwork, see M. McGinnis, *Designs of Faith: Essays and Paintings on World Religions* (CreateSpace Independent Publishing Platform, 2013).

22
Tierra Del Fuego

1. C. Darwin, "Climate and Production," in *Journal of Researches* (1845), p. 242, available at Wikisource: https://en.wikisource.org/wiki/Page:Darwin _Journal_of_Researches.djvu/264, accessed July 14, 2020. This story, told by anthropologist Anne MacKaye Chapman, who spent a great deal of time among the Haush, including accompanying them to the uninhabited island, brings the wind, waves, and rocks to life. See A. MacKaye Chapman, "Where the Seas Clash: The Land of the Ancient Haush, Tierra del Fuego," *Karukinka Cuadernos Fueguinos* 3–5 (1973). The English version can be found on the Reed Foundation's website, at thereedfoundation.org/rism/chapman /clash3.htm, accessed July 14, 2020.

2. Additional mythology can be found in C. Furlong, "The Haush and Ona, Primitive Tribes of Tierra del Fuego," *Proceedings of the 19th International Congress of Americanists*, ed. F. Hodge (Charleston, SC: Nabu Press, 2010), 432–444. The fickleness of nature is addressed in the Yaghan (from further west on the mainland) story of the ibis and the origin of glaciers. It comes from U. Calderón and C. Calderón, *Hai kur Mamašu shis (Quièro contarte un cuento)* (Valdivia, Chile: Ediciones Kultrún, 2005), 29–30. See also P. Grendi, trans., *Yaghan's Explorers and Settlers: 10,000 Years of Southern Tierra del Fuego Archipelago History* (museum permanent exhibit script), Martin Gusinde Anthropological Museum, Puerto Williams, Chile, 2008, 24.

Epilogue

1. Absent from Diodorus's creation story is a major step in the way contemporary science assesses nature's truths—testing. Validation techniques were not developed until the European Renaissance of the fifteenth century

CE. Modern science certifies its knowledge of the world by physically intervening, testing, and analyzing those aspects of nature's behavior that can be accessed by the (now techno-enhanced) senses. Scientists need to see for themselves—close up and in minute detail—whether the results of the tests they impose on nature support the ideas (we call them theories) they had proposed to explain what they observe. But what is deemed reasonable mustn't stray too far from the established norms of common sense. And if the tests fail, the theory needs to be altered and further tests devised. This is the so-called scientific method—the creed in which practitioners of science place their faith.

2. E. Thayer, ed., *The Library of Diodorus Siculus*, Loeb Classical Library (London: Heinemann, 1933), vol. 1, bk. 1.

3. Ibid., vol. 1, bk. 7, p. 1.

4. Ibid., vol. 1, bk. 7, p. 3.

5. Ibid., vol. 1, bk. 8, p. 8.

6. These words are my own.

Acknowledgments

I reiterate my thank you to Joe Calamia, former science and engineering editor at Yale University Press, for suggesting that I write this book along with its earlier companion, *Star Stories: Constellations and People*. He believed, as do I, in the value of promoting an approach to the study of world cosmologies that goes beyond those usually undertaken by scientists and science historians. This is my third book with Yale University Press wherein I have used the mindset and toolkit of cultural anthropology to explore how people acquire and express knowledge of their natural world.

I am especially grateful to Jean Thomson Black, Senior Executive Editor of Life Sciences, Physical Sciences, Environmental Sciences, and Medicine, for designing and carrying out the project with great enthusiasm and support. I also thank her skilled staff, especially editorial assistant Elizabeth Sylvia, production editor Susan Laity, and senior publicist Jennifer Doerr. Thanks, too, to indexer Alexa Selph.

Once again, skilled artist Matthew Green has perspicaciously employed his considerable talents to make my words come alive, and Erica Hanson and copyeditor Julie Carlson meticulously fact-checked and combed through the manuscript. Thanks to both of you as well.

My gratitude also goes out to many of my professional colleagues from the allied disciplines for helpful discussions of creation stories over the years, most especially Chris Vecsey and Carol Ann Lorenz from Native North American Studies, Gary Urton from Andean anthropology, Robert Garland from the Classics, and John MacDonald, whose work among the Inuit has enriched my perspective.

Last but not least, I thank my agent, Faith Hamlin, and her staff at Sanford Greenburger, for four decades of unflagging confidence in my work; my assistant, Diane Janney, for her skilled work preparing the manuscript; and Lorraine Aveni, for her inspiration and companionship in all my life ventures.

Index